Bestselling Authors and Business Leaders Praise *Aligned Thinking*

"I've always believed that life is a very special occasion—and special occasions are meant to be celebrated! Yet the pressures of life often leave us feeling too stressed to enjoy each day, let alone celebrate each moment. This book can change that. . . . Aligned Thinking has made a tremendous difference in my life. I invite you to open this book."

From the foreword by Ken Blanchard,
coauthor of *The One Minute Manager*®

"This warm and wonderful book shows you how to align every part of your life with your innermost values and your deepest convictions. It makes you a new person!"

Brian Tracy, author of the national
bestsellers *Eat That Frog!* and
*The 100 Absolutely Unbreakable Laws
of Business Success*

"To really get what you want, the first thing you'll want to get is this remarkable book."

Harvey Mackay, author of the
#1 *New York Times* bestseller
*Swim with the Sharks without
Being Eaten Alive*

"Voices like Steffen's are sorely needed today. This book will get you to think about your life and work in a holistic fashion."

Eric Tyson, author of
the national bestseller
Personal Finance for Dummies

"*Aligned Thinking* does more than just present time-proven principles of 'Aligned Thinking' for living life more fully—this book weaves thought-provoking guidelines into the fabric of a real-life story. Want to take charge of your life and live with more direction, meaning, and satisfaction? Begin by reading this practical, pragmatic book!"

Paul J. Meyer, founder of
Success Motivation International, Inc.,
and author of the *New York Times*
bestseller *Unlocking Your Legacy:
25 Keys to Success*

"I first learned of 'Aligned Thinking' as a General Motors dealer more than twenty years ago. I found it simple to use, especially when I thought I had too much to do. I have used it every day since to add more success and meaning to my life. *Aligned Thinking* has taken me to the next level. I will give copies to all my key clients so that I may share this wonderful gift. The book should become a classic."

Gary Polakoff, Financial Advisor,
Merrill Lynch

"*Aligned Thinking*, a very insightful approach to identifying how to truly make life a celebration and not drudgery."

Dan Wiersma, Senior Vice President
and General Manager,
Sony Professional Services

"This book will help to move you closer to your higher life purpose."

Dick Morton, Chief,
Classroom Operations,
Graduate School, USDA

"*Aligned Thinking* is a book I will have my staff read and also recommend to family and friends."

Jake Monaghan, Executive Director,
Customer Care, SBC

"A simple formula to help us experience a wonderful life. Written in a story format, the book is warm, loving, and gives us pause to internalize those 'golden nuggets.' Easy reading with a valuable message for everyone."

Roger Henson, retired Vice President,
Xerox Customer Service Operations

"Very empowering. . . . With the simple elegance of 'Aligned Thinking,' I have the freedom to celebrate life."

Mary P. Gai, editor and mother of four

"After I read Jim Steffen's *Aligned Thinking*, I knew I had to send copies to my clients. His book goes way beyond the masterful techniques for time management it provides. He uniquely shows how to create a life worth celebrating by focusing on what is most important to us. He tells us simply and powerfully how to 'do the right things right' in our personal and professional lives."

Emilio De Lia, professional coach
and retired AT&T executive

Aligned Thinking

Aligned Thinking

MAKE EVERY MOMENT COUNT

Jim Steffen

BERRETT-KOEHLER PUBLISHERS, INC.
San Francisco

Berrett-Koehler Publishers, Inc.
235 Montgomery Street, Suite 650
San Francisco, CA 94104-2916
Tel: (415) 288-0260   Fax: (415) 362-2512   www.bkconnection.com

Ordering Information
Quantity sales. Special discounts are available on quantity purchases by corporations, associations, and others. For details, contact the "Special Sales Department" at the Berrett-Koehler address above.

Individual sales. Berrett-Koehler publications are available through most bookstores. They can also be ordered directly from Berrett-Koehler: Tel: (800) 929-2929; Fax: (802) 864-7626; www.bkconnection.com

Orders for college textbook/course adoption use. Please contact Berrett-Koehler: Tel: (800) 929-2929; Fax: (802) 864-7626.

Orders by U.S. trade bookstores and wholesalers. Please contact Publishers Group West, 1700 Fourth Street, Berkeley, CA 94710. Tel: (510) 528-1444; Fax (510) 528-3444.

Berrett-Koehler and the BK logo are registered trademarks of Berrett-Koehler Publishers, Inc.

Printed in the United States of America

Berrett-Koehler books are printed on long-lasting acid-free paper. When it is available, we choose paper that has been manufactured by environmentally responsible processes. These may include using trees grown in sustainable forests, incorporating recycled paper, minimizing chlorine in bleaching, or recycling the energy produced at the paper mill.

Library of Congress Cataloging-in-Publication Data
Steffen, Jim.
    Aligned thinking : make every moment count : how successful
people get what they really want / Jim Steffen.
    p. cm. — (The Ken Blanchard series)
    ISBN-10: 1-57675-360-3 ISBN-13: 978-1-57675-360-6
    1. Success-Psychological aspects. 2. Goal (Psychology) I. Title
II. Series.
BF637.S8S6919 2005
158—dc22   2005050759

FIRST EDITION
10 09 08 07 06   10 9 8 7 6 5 4 3 2 1

Copyediting and proofreading by PeopleSpeak.
Book design and composition by Beverly Butterfield, Girl of the West Productions.

This book is dedicated to you, the reader,
and the people important to you.

When you discover the MIN Secret and use the
Aligned Thinking tools, you can make every moment
count and be on your way to getting what
you really want from life and work.

Many people have generously shared their problems and
insights with me in order to discover the MIN Secret
and the Aligned Thinking tools. I hope this book
makes it possible for you to generously share
them with those important to you.

It is my privilege to share with you
what I have been given.

To enjoy the full benefits of implementing
Aligned Thinking in your life, see the
author's gift at the end of the book.

CONTENTS

I'VE ALWAYS believed that life is a very special occasion—and special occasions are meant to be celebrated! Yet the pressures of life often leave us feeling too stressed to enjoy each day, let alone celebrate each moment. This book can change that.

Over twenty years ago I had the good fortune to take one of Jim Steffen's Aligned Thinking seminars. My book *The One Minute Manager* had just been published, and I was riding the wave of early success. It was an exciting time—but stressful, too. It seemed that I always had too much to do, too many interruptions, and too little control over my life and that I wasn't getting enough accomplished. Taking Jim's seminar was a turning point for me. Shortly afterward, I sent him a copy of my book with the following inscription:

> *To Jim,*
> *Thanks for sharing your wonderful time management system. If* The One Minute Manager *gets to be #1, the Aligned Thinking process will have played a major role. It already has made a difference in my life!*
>
> > *Best regards,*
> > *Ken Blanchard, August 1982*

Although I don't take personal credit for the phenomenal success of *The One Minute Manager* (to date the book has sold over thirteen million copies in twenty-seven languages), Jim's teaching certainly helped me to stay focused and appreciate each day.

In his profound book, Jim reveals the secrets of Aligned Thinking. As you walk in the shoes of Ray and Carol Walters, you will discover how to define and live your ideal professional and personal life. You'll also learn how to overcome the frustration of too much to do, increase accomplishment and satisfaction, reduce stress, get rid of interruptions, and feel more freedom, meaning, and serenity in your life. If you have a significant other, Aligned Thinking will help you have fun together and grow closer. For your organization, it will increase productivity, motivation, and morale. For your clients, it will empower you to deliver better service and increase satisfaction and loyalty.

Many people believe that they could never align every action with what they really want. The story of Ray and Carol Walters will show you why this belief is a myth. Aligned Thinking has made a tremendous difference in my life. I invite you to open this book and learn the answers to the three Life Aligning Questions that lead to the discovery of the MIN Secret, which will help you to live your dreams. Your life is a special occasion, and it's time to start celebrating!

KEN BLANCHARD
San Diego, California

AS I was writing this book, people asked me three questions. Here are the questions and their answers.

The first question is, What can I expect from Aligned Thinking? Aligned Thinking will help you do what most believe impossible: align *every action* with what you *really* want. Because of this, if your experience is similar to that of thousands who have discovered and use Aligned Thinking, you can expect a quantum leap in the following areas:

1 Overcoming the frustration of too much to do

2 Increasing accomplishment and satisfaction

3 Reducing stress and interruptions

In addition, Aligned Thinking offers at least three bonus benefits for the people important to you. For your organization, Aligned Thinking will help you increase productivity, motivation, and morale. For your clients, you will be able to deliver better service and establish higher levels of satisfaction and loyalty. Finally, for you and your significant other, Aligned Thinking will give you a process by which to have fun growing closer together.

The second question is, Where did Aligned Thinking—the process—come from? I interviewed over three thousand managers about maximizing their leadership effectiveness. Before I met with them, I had them complete profiles and plans for their own professional improvement. In the interview, I learned what they really wanted from both life and work and how the successful ones got what they *really* wanted. A summary of the best tools became the Aligned Thinking process.

Over time, I had the opportunity to share these insights with people from 140 Fortune 500 companies (for the list, go to www.SSAinternational.com). I have to thank those people for their help in making the process

- Quicker to learn
- Easier to remember—some have used it daily for more than twenty years
- Simpler to use—just a nine-word MIN Secret
- All-inclusive—it applies 24/7 both professionally and personally

The third question is, What's the story behind *Aligned Thinking*, the book? Ken Blanchard helped me get my doctorate at the University of Massachusetts in 1972. Ten years later, just after *The One Minute Manager* was published, he attended an Aligned Thinking seminar. The seminar helped Ken focus on making his book the bestseller it is. Shortly thereafter, he suggested writing this book.

Over the next twenty years, I tried three times with over fifteen drafts to write this book by myself. My success was zero. Frustrated and out of options, I turned to my Higher Spirit.

Immediately, but oh so slowly, changes began to occur. The changes all seemed so natural, but after each change, progress was made! Literary agent Carol Mann said the first proposal for the book was terrible. After listening to the sad twenty-year history of the book, she insightfully insisted, "Ken Blanchard helped you; you helped him. Now together you need to help others."

Ken agreed to help. At exactly the right time, he discovered Martha Lawrence, editor par excellence, who did marvelous things with the manuscript. At just the right time, Steve Piersanti of Berrett-Koehler appeared and helped us to bring out the simple elegance of Aligned Thinking. So many coincidences just seemed to happen at the right time. However, as Martha has said many times, "Jim, there are no coincidences."

Your reading this book is no coincidence. When you understand and answer the three Life Aligning Questions and discover the MIN Secret, you will have a tool set you can use for the rest of your life. Judging from my thirty years of experience, I believe this tool set will help you successfully make every moment count, so you can daily, even moment-by-moment, move closer on your journey to what you *really* want.

I'm honored and delighted to share with you what I have been so generously given.

JIM STEFFEN
December 2005

Aligned
Thinking

PART ONE

Discovering the
MIN Secret

CHAPTER ONE

The Black Tunnel

Too much to do! I never get everything done!
Too many interruptions!
Not enough time with the family!
So little control over my life!
Life doesn't seem to have much meaning anymore.

THESE WERE Ray's thoughts as the train from Lower Manhattan tunneled to New Jersey under the Hudson River. As Ray looked out the window into the blackness, an occasional light flashed by to show him how dark the tunnel truly was.

How fitting, he thought. *This is like my life. I feel like I'm in a dark tunnel. My life is underwater.* The infrequent flashes of light reminded him of the few lights in his life—his wife, Carol, and their two children. Unfortunately, as with the lights flashing by, he saw them for all too short a time.

What have I really accomplished today? Ray took out his organizer and reviewed the day. He'd skipped lunch and stayed late at work. He added two things he'd forgotten to put on his to-do list. This made the list longer than it had been at the beginning of the day. He felt miserable.

In frustrating times like these, his wife was his beacon of hope. When he talked over problems with Carol, she always helped him come up with solutions. What a great partner he had! He resolved that he'd discuss his dark, underwater life with her tonight.

Ray looked at his watch. *Nine o'clock already.* Dinner would be over and the kids would be in their rooms working on their homework. The thought angered him. He pounded the time organizer as if it were the cause.

Life is too long on work and too short on real meaning, Ray thought. The muscles in his neck felt so tight they hurt. He couldn't wait for Carol to help.

"I need things to change!" he declared.

CHAPTER TWO

An Unwelcome Surprise

AS RAY walked to his car from the train, he called Carol on his cell phone to let her know he was on his way home. She sounded a bit distracted but told him she would be very glad to see him.

Once home and settled in, Ray reviewed his frustrations and anger with Carol. He fully expected that she would listen sympathetically. With her experienced help, he would create a specific plan to solve the problems.

Ray had just started his list of frustrations when Carol interrupted.

"Too much to do? Tell me about it!" she fumed. He wasn't prepared for this. Instead of a supportive ear, he got an earful.

"I was up with you at six," she said. "As soon as the kids were off to school, I was off to work. You know I hate to have them come home before me. Even though they're older now, it's still not okay. When I got home today, they were both doing their homework, which is great. But I had to take Tammy to her music lesson, do shopping, spend time on my own paperwork, and then go back to pick her up. As if that weren't enough, I needed to interrupt it to get Jamie to and from baseball."

Carol was on a roll. It was obvious that she also needed support.

"Work was full of interruptions interrupted by interruptions," she continued. "Our lives are empty! There's too little family time, too little control, not enough getting accomplished, and too little real meaning!"

With the flood of anxiety Carol was dumping out, Ray couldn't get a word in.

"Ray, what's happened to our dreams? We wanted to have daily family time and family weekends a few times a year. And what about alone time for us? This isn't our dream! It's a nightmare!"

Carol was close to tears. Finally, Ray saw an opening and said quickly, "You're right! We have to change if we want to take control and live our dreams. I wish my dad were still alive. He was usually busy with business, but when he was home, he'd help me think through problems. When he retired at sixty-two, he'd planned to spend more time with Mom and us kids. But he died just a year later."

"Let's not let that happen to us," Carol said.

Ray paused a moment and just looked at his wife. "Tonight, when I was in that black tunnel under the Hudson, I tried to figure out when all this started. What happened to the dreams we had before we were married?"

Carol shrugged. "I don't know."

"I think . . . ," Ray hesitated, struggling for words, "the trouble started as early as our honeymoon. Remember how I had a hard time relaxing on that glorious beach? I couldn't just enjoy the sun and sand . . . or even you. I had to check the stock market almost every hour. There were three of us on our honeymoon: you, me, and my work!"

"Four of us!" Carol sighed. "I wasn't exactly the blissful bride. I had just landed my first managerial position. I couldn't let go, either. I called the office at least ten times during that week, when I didn't have to."

"How can we get rid of all this meaningless stress?" said Ray. "Who do we know who really seems to have their life together?"

The question hung in the air.

The silence thundered!

He restated the question. "Who do we know who has found great meaning in life?"

Carol's eyes lit up. "That sounds like Ed and Alanna! They have five kids, and one of their sons is mentally handicapped. On top of everything, Alanna finds time to distribute goods to the poor."

"You're right," said Ray. "Ed seems so centered, and yet he's got his hands full with a very successful company. He hasn't exactly had it easy, either. One of his key employees started a business behind his back. The guy used Ed's salespeople to sell to Ed's own clients. He charged Ed's clients and put the fees in his own pocket, the whole time drawing a salary from Ed. He even used Ed's copier to copy his invoices. That's how Ed caught him."

"Talk about stress," said Carol.

Ray nodded. "Yeah, it messed up Ed's business for a while. But no matter what's going on, Ed always seems to find great meaning in his life. He and Alanna have a glow about them, like they're connected to some tremendous, hidden power. I want to know what that is."

"I'm sure they'd be willing to share some ideas with us," said Carol.

"Would you call them tomorrow?" Ray held up a hand. "No, wait. You're busy enough. I'll make the arrangements."

That night in bed, Carol laid her head on Ray's shoulder, the way she slept many a night. It was reassuring. Yes, she truly was his beacon of hope in the dark tunnel. He got the feeling that the train was starting to slow down. Ray, not an overly religious man, let a little "Thank God" slip out.

CHAPTER THREE

Aligned Thinking Offers Hope

THAT SATURDAY evening at their favorite restaurant, Ray and Carol met Ed and Alanna for dinner. As soon as they ordered their meal, Carol—being the action-oriented person she was—related the entire situation: the frustration of too much to do, too many interruptions, and too little meaning in their lives.

Ray added, "Carol astounded me. In some areas, her situation was worse than mine. We asked ourselves, Who among our friends seem to have their lives together, and how do they do it? We thought of the two of you. You seem to have some secret power we'd like to know about."

Ed smiled. "Thanks, guys. It wasn't always this easy. Alanna and I used to have the same feelings and problems that you do, like too much to do and too little meaning in life. Then we attended a workshop led by Coach Eric. He was our soccer coach in school, Ray. Remember?"

Ray nodded. "Sure. Never had a coach who was more positive and encouraging. We won a lot of championships with Coach Eric, didn't we?"

"Yep," said Ed. "Turns out Coach's business is giving productivity seminars to Fortune 500 companies. He helps people get what they really want from life and work by guiding them to become Aligned Thinkers. He's highly successful at it. Thanks to Coach, Alanna and I learned how to live as Aligned Thinkers."

"Aligned Thinkers?" Carol looked dubious. "What's an Aligned Thinker? I've never heard that term before. Is becoming an Aligned Thinker complicated?"

"No. It's easy to learn and even easier to use," Ed added quickly. "Becoming an Aligned Thinker depends on a set of tools that will help you discover the MIN Secret."

"What's the MIN Secret?" Ray asked.

"MIN stands for 'most important now,'" Ed replied. "It's an amazing concept that can be used by anyone: homemakers, students, retirees, and businesspeople. It will help you make every moment count. When that happens, you are well on your way to getting what you really want. The wonderful thing about Coach's Aligned Thinking tools is that they provide a powerful, proven solution to all the frustrations you and Carol are experiencing."

"Hate to be a skeptic," Carol said, "but I find this hard to believe."

"It's true," Alanna responded calmly. "Your situation sounds like ours fifteen years ago. At first I didn't believe I could live as an Aligned Thinker, not with five kids! But once I applied Coach's simple tools, I went from living a nightmare existence—with all the frustrations you're expressing—to being an Aligned Thinker, living my dreams."

Carol shook her head. "If something seems too good to be true, it usually is. Alanna, if I didn't know you better, I'd think you were putting us on. Make *every* moment count? With a job, husband, and two kids—I wish!"

Alanna replied, "Coach has a way of making difficult things simple. When he described what an Aligned Thinker is, we questioned whether it was remotely possible to live that way. But Coach Eric made believers out of us by showing us step-by-step how to become Aligned Thinkers. We proved to ourselves that we could really have the life we wanted, even with five kids plus." She turned to her husband. "Ed, you can draw. Show them the Aligned Thinker circle."

Ed drew on a napkin and said, "You are an Aligned Thinker when . . . what you *really* want from life and work drives every action, and . . . *every* action takes you, step-by-step, back to what you really want."

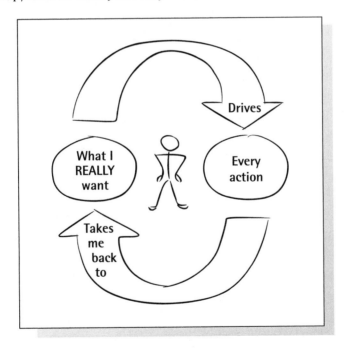

Ray and Carol studied the drawing. The more they studied, the more skeptical they looked. "Every action? Do you really mean every single action?" Carol asked.

Alanna smiled confidently. "I knew the definition would cause doubts. That 'every' is both the beauty and the simplicity of it."

"At first, I was also very skeptical," Ed added. "Once Coach shared the three Life Aligning Questions that impact everyone's life every day and showed us how to answer them, we discovered the MIN Secret. We found we could align *every action* with what we really want."

Alanna added before Ray or Carol could respond, "I was amazed that with five kids, I could be aligned with *every* action. The Aligned Thinking tools, especially the MIN Secret, make it simpler than I could imagine."

This was too much for Carol. "MIN Secret? Three Life Aligning Questions to answer? What is this MIN Secret? What are the three questions that can help you align every action with what you really want?"

Ed smiled at Alanna. Alanna smiled back. Then Ed said very politely, "Would you mind if Coach Eric answered your questions? With his years of experience, he found the MIN Secret is more valuable to people if they discover it themselves as they experience the answers to the three questions. He asked us not to share the MIN Secret so people could discover it themselves. Would you mind if we respect his wish?"

There was a short pause. Then Ed added, "I can say that the secret power you mentioned Alanna and I have is partly due to the fact that all our actions are aligned with what we *really* want."

This stopped Ray and Carol. They were very curious about the last statement. They wanted to ask more. However, Ed had so politely requested that they honor Coach Eric's request, how could they do otherwise?

Driving home that night, Ray said, "I'm going to call Coach Eric in the morning. Even before we met tonight, I knew Ed and Alanna had something special. They sure do have their lives together, and now I'm really curious about how they do it. Although I have my doubts about this Aligned Thinking stuff, I trust Coach Eric. I see some light at the end of this black tunnel we're in—and it's not just another train coming."

The next morning Ray made a life-changing phone call.

"Hi, Coach Eric, it's Ray Walters. Remember me?"

"Of course I do!" said Coach warmly. "You and Stew had a great soccer give-and-go. It was always a pleasure watching you two."

Ray told Coach about his and Carol's frustrations, their talk with Alanna and Ed, their desire for the benefits of living as Aligned Thinkers, and their deep doubts that they could live that way. He finally asked Coach if he would guide them.

"Sure," said Coach. "Let's meet this weekend. All I ask is that you and Carol make a list of four or five goals that you'd like to accomplish by living as Aligned Thinkers and bring it with you. This list should be so complete that when you and Carol achieve all the goals on it, you'll be living your ideal professional and personal life."

This was much more than Ray had expected. With disbelief he said, "Could you repeat that? I'm not sure I heard you correctly."

"You heard me right," said Coach. "See you this weekend."

CHAPTER FOUR

Defining Your Ideal Professional and Personal Life

✺ ON A beautiful day in early June—unusually warm after a bitter cold spring in the New York–New Jersey area—Ray and Carol drove to Coach Eric's home. Ray thought that maybe their list of professional and personal ideals was too much to ask for. Even so, he had high hopes. He heard the tune "June Is Busting Out All Over" playing in his head and felt the warm sun of hope shining in his heart.

Coach Eric greeted Ray and Carol warmly. He invited them in for refreshments and listened as they gave him a recap of the frustrations they'd shared with Ed and Alanna.

"Ed and Alanna are two of my favorite people," Coach said with a twinkle in his eye. "How much did they tell you about Aligned Thinking?"

Ray shared all that Ed and Alanna had told them. Then Carol added, "We are very curious about this Aligned Thinking that Ed and Alanna say is the key to their happiness. And we are both skeptical that we can align every action with what we really want."

Coach smiled and said, "Great! That's a great place to be in. Let me ask you not to worry about aligning every action. Years ago, before my clients helped me discover Aligned Thinking, I never dreamed I could align every action. And at the time I was not clear about what I really wanted."

Carol and Ray found this reassuring. Coach continued. "Let me see your list of what you want in your ideal professional and personal life."

Ray handed him their list and said rather apologetically, "I hope we are not asking for too much."

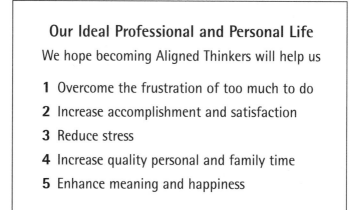

Our Ideal Professional and Personal Life

We hope becoming Aligned Thinkers will help us

1 Overcome the frustration of too much to do

2 Increase accomplishment and satisfaction

3 Reduce stress

4 Increase quality personal and family time

5 Enhance meaning and happiness

Coach nodded approvingly. "There's nothing here that becoming an Aligned Thinker can't give you. I do have one request though. Would you add 'make every moment count so life becomes a celebration' to the list?"

Ray added the line and Coach continued, "When you understand the three questions that impact everyone daily and discover the MIN Secret, it will help you live your ideal professional and personal life or better. You'll also be able to do some things most people find hard to believe, like achieve everything you plan each day and get rid of all interruptions." With this, Ray and Carol were even more skeptical. However, their hope mounted with their skepticism.

With confidence, Coach continued, "But one step at a time. Let's agree that if you feel you can't do a step, you will immediately tell the person you're working with. You'll go on only when you're comfortable with the present step."

"Hard to believe, but agreed," Ray said. Carol nodded with disbelief.

"Then let's get started!" Coach said with a smile.

CHAPTER FIVE

The Aligned Thinking Pyramid

COACH INVITED Ray and Carol to sit with him around a big oak table. When they were settled, he said, "Over the years, thousands of businesspeople I coached helped me identify three Life Aligning Questions. The interesting thing is these three questions impact everyone's life, whether they know it or not. Our goal has been to make it quicker, easier, and simpler: quicker to learn the Aligned Thinking tools that help answer the three questions, easier to remember the tools, and simpler to get what you *really* want from life.

"As we agreed, it is important that you focus on just one of the questions at a time. Answering the first of these critical life-impacting questions will lead you to the next one.

"Here is an illustration that shows how the three questions build, leading to the MIN Secret. The MIN Secret is the key to your living as an Aligned Thinker, 24/7."

Coach pulled out an eye-catching illustration and handed it to Ray and Carol.

Aligned Thinking Pyramid

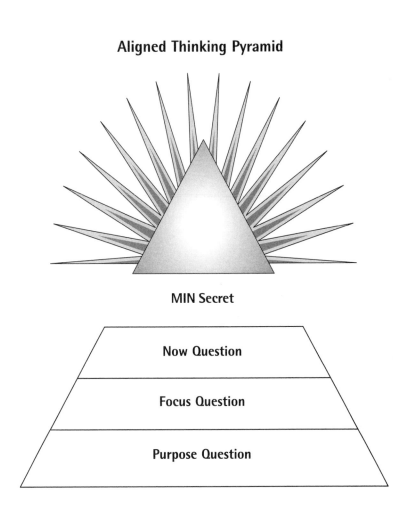

MIN Secret

| Now Question |
| Focus Question |
| Purpose Question |

Ray spoke with some concern. "It looks simple enough. But is it?"

Coach answered with calm confidence, "When you understand how to answer the three questions and live the answers, you'll discover the MIN Secret. At this point my clients say, 'Why, this is just common sense.'

"The thing is," Coach continued, "you don't get any benefits from mere common sense. The only time you get benefits is when you make common sense common practice.

"To make it easy, I will arrange for you to visit two couples and a single mother. An important part of Aligned Thinking is what you discover when you implement it yourself. Each will share the insights they have personally gained. If you agree, you will make one visit a week. Between visits I would like you to practice the insights they share with you.

"When you take one question at a time, you will learn the insights that make answering and living the answer easy. It will be like riding a bike."

Carol looked puzzled. "Like riding a bike?"

"Yes," Coach assured her. "When you learn to ride a bike, you master three things—steering, pedaling, and balancing. When you begin, if you try all three at once, you will probably fall more often than necessary. However, if you just guide first and let someone else balance and move you, it's easier. Then you add the pedaling yourself. Finally, your helper or coach lets you balance also. Once you get all three, you never forget how to ride a bike. You might be rusty, but you can pick it up quickly.

"The three questions of Aligned Thinking and using the MIN Secret are the same. Once you get it, you never forget it. I have clients who have used the MIN Secret daily, even moment-by-moment, for more than twenty-five years."

Ray and Carol were intrigued by the bike example but more intrigued by someone using the MIN Secret daily for twenty-five years.

CHAPTER SIX

Life Aligning Question One

THE PURPOSE QUESTION

COACH INTERRUPTED Ray and Carol's musing with, "Ready for the next step?"

"Sure!" Ray said. Carol nodded her approval.

Coach Eric continued. "Listening to the things that upset you, I understand that one of the most frustrating is that life—especially your work life—doesn't seem to have much meaning anymore. Do I have that correct?"

"Correct!" Carol responded with emphasis.

"Good," Coach said. "I'm going to send you to Mary and Mike Hall. At one time they had so little meaning in their work lives that they were both ready to quit their jobs. Today they're masters at living a life full of meaning. I'm sure they'll be glad to share their journey with you. Could you two free your schedules to meet with them this Saturday?"

"Definitely!" said Carol with enthusiasm.

"Great!" Coach responded. "In Mary and Mike, you will find an exceptional example of how ordinary people can be very successful getting what they really want, in this case a very meaningful life starting with work."

"Starting with work? What's that mean?" asked Ray.

"Mary and Mike will show you. Remember, implementation is the key. Mary and Mike have discovered a lot to share," said Coach with a smile.

The next Saturday evening, Ray and Carol pulled up to Mary and Mike Hall's modest home. As they walked to the door, Carol commented on what a clean, well-cared-for look the house had.

Mike Hall met them with a warm smile. "Come in, you guys. Mary and I have been looking forward to meeting you."

Mike was tall with silver hair, and he appeared to be in fine health. Ray wondered how he stayed so fit.

Mary welcomed them with a smile. "We're so honored that Coach Eric asked you to visit us first. What a difference implementing Aligned Thinking has made in our lives! Come on in and make yourselves comfortable."

While Mike and Mary brought out drinks and snacks, they talked and laughed with Ray and Carol.

"You two do look happy," Ray commented.

Mary laughed. "It wasn't always this way. There was a time when we were totally fed up with our lives, especially work."

"What changed?" asked Carol, immediately searching for answers.

"To explain, I have to go back to when all the kids were in school. We figured that with the expense of college coming, I needed to return to work. Before the kids, I was a nurse in a hospital. I loved helping people. Now the hospital was looking for a head nurse on one of the floors, so I applied and got the job. To increase his income, Mike accepted the service manager's position at the dealership where he worked."

Mike picked up the story. "I really enjoyed fixing cars. I would have stayed in that job, but the boss said if I wanted to get the raise I asked for, I needed to take the manager's job he'd offered me twice before. He said I would be great at it and talked me into giving it a six-month trial. For financial considerations, I finally gave in. Immediately life went downhill."

Mike paused. "No, not just downhill; more like crash and burn!"

"I could see Mike change," Mary added. "He began yelling at the kids, which he rarely did before. At the same time, I was suffering in my new job. As a nurse, I had loved to get up in the morning to help people get well. But it was different as a head nurse. Not only did I have to deal with patients, but I had to deal with doctors, visitors, regulations, employees, and other nurses as well. That wasn't my thing. I didn't even enjoy getting up in the morning anymore."

Ray and Carol nodded their heads. Mary's story felt familiar.

"So what did you do?" Carol asked.

Mary blushed slightly and said, "This is the part Coach doesn't know about. It's not what we recommend, but since it might help you understand how down we were and how Aligned Thinking helped us, here's what happened. Mike came home one night and yelled at the kids. Later, with a heavy heart, I said, 'Mike, you're changing.' Then he started yelling at me. For about four minutes, we went at it. He shouted, 'You're changing, too!'

"I shouted back, 'If you had my job, you'd understand! If I just didn't have any patients, my job would be easy!'

"Mike just stared at me and slowly began to smile. I stopped yelling and thought about what I'd just said. If there were no patients in my hospital, I wouldn't have a job! I realized how ridiculous I'd sounded. We both started to laugh. We agreed that we would have a heart-to-heart talk right then and there."

"I went first," said Mike. "I complained about how my frustrations started in the morning with irritated car owners. Things got worse from there with the phones ringing, mechanics with this or that problem, customers upset about their bills, slow workers, and parts that weren't available. There were too many interruptions. And too much stress!"

"I can relate to that," Ray said. Carol nodded her agreement.

"I went next," said Mary. "As head nurse in charge of my floor, I had treatments to give, medicines to distribute, employees to supervise, doctors to keep happy, emergencies to deal with, and patients and their families to talk with. My days consisted of interruptions interrupted by interruptions. Talking about it with Mike that day just upset me more."

Ray and Carol were leaning forward, relating to each frustration. "That sounds all too familiar," said Carol. "How did you solve these problems? You seem so happy and calm now."

Mary continued, "Our first solutions weren't good ones. We decided that Mike and I were just not cut out to lead. We wanted the money so we could send our kids to good colleges, but we figured it was not meant to be. We decided to back off from that dream. Since Mike's six-month trial period was ending, he planned to resign. I also planned to step down as head nurse of the floor. Things were so bad, giving up our cherished dreams was a relief."

Mike nodded. "I went to our dealership's owner and told him I wanted my old job back. I shared with him how Mary and I felt. He said I could have my old job back because that was his promise, but he asked Mary and me to attend Coach's

Aligned Thinking workshop first. We didn't like the idea, but we agreed to go. Thank God we did. Our nightmare turned into a dream."

"This is the binder we kept from that workshop," Mary said as she placed a book on the coffee table. "I think you two will be especially interested in the first of the Life Aligning Questions. This is the question that helped us realign our lives." She pointed to a page from the seminar notes.

The Purpose Question
∎

*What do I **really** want from life and work?*

"So this is the purpose question on Coach's Aligned Thinking pyramid," Ray said. "How do you figure out what you *really* want? Simple as that question is, with so many life pressures, it's hard to know for sure."

"Coach's tools really helped," said Mary. "First, we wrote our own eulogies, with emphasis on how we would like to be remembered."

"That must have been challenging," said Ray.

"It was," said Mary. "But very insightful, like opening the door into my heart. My first 'aha' was that Mike and I had lost sight of our original life purpose. Coach pointed out that the meaning of our daily actions comes from their purpose. With Mike and me, since there was no alignment between our daily actions and what we wanted from our life or work, we were starved for meaning. Working harder only made matters worse. Coach also pointed out that this lack of alignment causes problems for most people."

"So what did you write in your eulogy?" Carol asked Mary.

"I wrote, I would like people to say that I really cared about them as people and that I had the skill, attitude, and energy to help many of them.' As a young girl, I always enjoyed helping people. When it came time to pick a career, I felt helping others as a nurse would be a great life's work. But in my job as head nurse, I couldn't connect the incessant demands with my life purpose. All I saw were interruptions interrupted by interruptions."

"My situation was similar," Mike added. "I was looking for a similar accomplishment in my eulogy. As a young man, I thought of going into the priesthood or the Peace Corps. But I enjoyed fixing cars and was good at it. So I became a mechanic to help people by fixing their cars. As a service manager, I couldn't see how all the interruptions I dealt with were helping people. I could not connect my daily actions to my vision and values. I only saw the interruptions as interruptions. When I didn't connect my actions to what I really wanted from life, the actions lost meaning. My life became a void. I wanted out."

"I can relate," said Ray.

"My first 'aha' was similar to Mary's, only I would say it a little differently. We were miserable. We had huge bomb craters where our inner fulfillment should have been and couldn't understand why. We just did not understand the nature of inner fulfillment. We wanted to do good things for people—Mary by helping them get well, me by fixing their cars."

"So what was the problem?" asked Carol.

"Basically, we couldn't connect our everyday actions with our original purpose of helping others. Answering this first Life Aligning Question helped me focus on what I really wanted from life—to help people. Eventually, Aligned Thinking showed me how to make the connection between my daily actions and the life I dreamed of living. That awareness brought into focus that the *interruptions at work were really opportunities.*"

Ray and Carol wondered how Mike had made that connection.

"Before I was an Aligned Thinker, if one of my mechanics came to me demanding this or that, I would see him as a troublemaker. Once I aligned my thinking, I could see that he was really just calling for help. When a customer is upset, he or she is really saying, 'I'm frustrated. I need your special help.' Slowly—ever so slowly—I began to realize I had more opportunities to help people as the service manager than I ever had as a mechanic. As I saw how my actions aligned me step-by-step with my true life purpose, the very actions that had sapped my energy before now gave me new energy. Today, there is nothing that gives me more energy than seeing myself as a successful person doing what I really want, which is helping people."

"Even though it is the same job?" asked Carol. "How come?"

"Because activities that give life meaning also give 'here and now' energy," Mike replied.

Ray grabbed a pen and piece of paper. "Mike, would you say that again? I want to make a note of it."

As Mike repeated the words, Ray jotted them down:

Activities that give life meaning also give "here and now" energy.

Mike continued. "My boss pointed out how much I'd accomplished. He said I'd created a fourfold win. First, *his* win was keeping me in the position. Second, I treated clients much better once I saw their problems as opportunities—the clients win. Third, this translated into repeat business and greater profits—the company wins. Fourth, because I used the mechanics' needs as opportunities to serve them, I improved their morale and they became more motivated—the mechanics win. My boss was right: it was a quadruple win."

"There was another win, too," said Mary with a smile. "When Mike was just going through the motions at work and not feeling connected to his life purpose, he came home exhausted and cranky. He even looked older."

"I was a bear," Mike said with a laugh. "I yelled at everyone. Nonaligned living was taking years off my life. I felt terrible most of the time."

"You look great today," said Carol.

"Thanks. People tell me I look young for fifty-nine. I'm a living example. Because what I do is taking me to where I want to be, I can love what I do. It keeps me young."

"I heard you saying two things," Ray said. "First, clarify your purpose and what you really want from work. You did it by writing what you would like to hear in your eulogy. Second, make certain your actions at work are connected to what you really want—in other words, what is meaningful to you. Would you say I've captured what you've been telling us?"

"I would say you're close," Mike replied. "But I would add, 'Make certain *every* action takes you back to what you *really* want.' Mary and I started with work but eventually connected all our actions to our life purpose, including what we did in our personal life. If an action doesn't take you back to your purpose, why do it?"

"That's a good question," Ray said slowly as he considered it. "Coach said you started out with being aligned in work, but he didn't say where you went from there. So you went to the personal and covered everything?"

"That's the simplicity of it," Mike said. "Eventually, you'll see how the simple elegance of the MIN Secret helps you be aligned 24/7."

"Simplicity?" Carol said with a frown. *"Give me a break!"*

CHAPTER SEVEN

How to Clarify Your Life Purpose

WHAT IS it, Carol?" Mike asked. "You look troubled."

"Ray's summary might be simple, but I hardly think answering the question about my life purpose—What do I really want?—is simple. It would be great if someone could come up with a simple way to answer the question."

"As a matter of fact," Mike replied, "Somebody has. Coach gave us a simple method to answer that question in just three steps."

"How can a question like that ever be simple?" asked Carol.

"Most people have never written their life purpose," Mike replied, "partly because it is a very challenging thing to do. Coach's three-step method makes it possible to do in just fifteen to thirty minutes. The key to his method is to just do one step at a time.

"What Mary and I liked about it was the simplicity of each step taken one at a time. When we had completed the three steps, we had clarified our purpose and created a life mission that we could use daily. And we did it in priority order, which helps when there are several options, which is often the case. The first time is challenging but very interesting. After that, Coach encouraged us to return to our mission every three months to refine it. Each time we refined it, we got clearer about what we really wanted from life and work."

Mike produced a copy of a page from the book Coach had given him.

Aligned Thinking Three-Step Method to Clarify the Purpose Question:

What Do I Really Want from Life and Work?

Step 1: Capture your values, desires, and needs.
If you could have just one item below, what would it be? Circle it.

Appreciation of arts	Person I want to be
Career	Physical well-being
Contribution to humanity	Retirement
Entertainment	Serving others
Family	Spiritual well-being
Financial well-being	Spouse/significant other
Friends	Travel
Home	Other_____
Intellectual well-being	Other_____

Step 2: Create your prioritized personal purpose.

A. Related to this one item, *what* do you want and *why*? Write your answer.

B. If you could have just one more item, what would it be? Circle it; then repeat A.

C. Repeat A and B until you have exhausted what you really want. (Caution: the more items you want, the more difficult it is to focus on one.)

Step 3: Review your purpose daily; refine it quarterly.
Create a funday for purpose—for example, a fun two-hour meeting in some nice place—each quarter to refine your purpose. The funday for purpose must be a special anticipated event.

As Carol and Ray studied the three-step method, Mike said, "The first step helps you capture your values. The process of picking just one area at a time really helps you focus and makes it much easier. The second step of writing what you want and why helps you prioritize what you want in life. The third step—which has been the most helpful for me— is to review your purpose daily and refine it quarterly."

"Tell them about the funday for purpose," Mary said.

"It's one of Coach's most useful ideas," Mike replied. "As the name indicates, it's fun. You take turns being the funday planner. The planner arranges a time and a fun place where you can be alone and free for at least two hours to focus on refining your life purpose and goals."

Mary nodded, remembering. "At first, it was just two hours with a meal. In time, our funday for purpose stretched into a weekend. It's always a great time. Mike and I compete with each other for who can plan the best weekend. We have some wonderful memories."

"So," said Carol, who was still studying the three-step method, "Why is it important to create my life purpose in priority order?"

Mike was quick to answer. "For me, following the step of picking the most important value, then the next most important, has done two things. First, it made capturing my values easier. Second, when I finished the process, I had my priorities in order. That order is really helpful to me when I'm deciding what to do next. I have the priority order of my life purpose to help me decide.

"Coach suggested we give you a copy of our life purpose to give you some ideas. At first, our purposes were different. Over time, they converged. Here is a copy for each of you to keep."

Mary and Mike's Life Purpose
(revised many times)

Purpose in Priority Order	The "Why"
1 Create a great relationship with our **Higher Spirit**	• Our Higher Spirit has given us so much; it is our privilege to love Him. • This great relationship will give our actions in this life more meaning **now**. • If we mess up everything else but get this straight, we are okay for eternity.
2 Serve others starting with **spouse and family**	Our number two responsibility in life is to love others, especially beginning at home.
3 Serve others in **our work**	This is where we spend the most time and have the most opportunities to serve.
4 Serve others in the **volunteer sector**	Many of God's children need what we can offer.
5 Create **financial security**	This is not critical but very helpful for doing all the above.
6 Enjoy **entertainment**	This adds spice to life. We want to emphasize family fun, like skiing and travel.
7 Provide for **retirement**	We want to save for the future but also plan to be very active so retirement brings optimal inner fulfillment.

CHAPTER EIGHT

Living the Answer to the Purpose Question

RAY SAID to Mary and Mike, "Coach Eric told us how important it is to implement the Aligned Thinking tools. We appreciate your sharing your insights so generously and especially value the copy of your life purpose."

"You can borrow whatever you want," Mary said. "We borrowed freely from Coach and some of the people who helped us."

"We'll do that," Carol replied. On the way home, Carol and Ray agreed that the next morning they would devote the first two hours after church to answering the purpose question.

The following summer day dawned clear and turned into a glorious Sunday. The deck was a warm, peaceful place in the late morning. As planned, Carol and Ray created their own life purposes.

Thirty minutes later they compared purposes. They discovered they had both borrowed generously from Mike and Mary, with some variations. Carol proposed, "I don't think it's critical that our life purposes or missions be the same. I think we should agree it's okay to be different."

Ray agreed and added, "I suggest with differences, we ask how we can support the other person getting what they want."

They agreed to review their purposes each morning and to focus each of their actions during the day toward their purposes.

On Wednesday evening after the kids were in their rooms, Ray and Carol shared a quiet moment. Ray asked Carol, "How's becoming an Aligned Thinker going?"

"I've made progress, but I'm experiencing some challenges," Carol replied. "Each morning, as promised, I have reviewed the mission I created. Then I reviewed my to-do list for the day to come."

"And?" Ray asked.

Carol summarized, "I'm on my way. I definitely got more done. And my accomplishments had more meaning because I saw how they were taking me back to what I really wanted. However, there is too big a gap between my mission and what I will do in the moment. And I still am miles away from getting everything done."

"I had a similar result," Ray replied. "Reviewing my mission only took a minute each morning. My to-do's became more aligned with what I really want in life.

"Mike told us we should align every action—both professional and personal—with what we really want. With clients, a boss, employees, kids, and a wife," he smiled at Carol, "I still don't see how I am free in all I do to align every action with what I really want. I need tools or insights to solve this problem and tools for a better business-personal balance."

On Friday evening around the big oak table, Coach listened to their progress toward being more aligned.

"I notice the frustration you're experiencing, Carol, about having too large a gap between your mission and the moment. I also notice your anxiety, Ray, about not being free to align every action and your desire for better balance in your business and personal life.

"Your frustrations tell me you're ready to meet the next person," Coach declared.

CHAPTER NINE

How to Be Free in Every Action

"THE PERSON you will meet tomorrow is a real master of the art of feeling free with *every action* in the midst of a busy, very challenging life," Coach told Ray and Carol. "Eleanor Mitchell is a retired golf champion, a very successful entrepreneur, a CEO, and a single mother of two. Eleanor and her husband built their company together. He loved piloting his own plane. He died in a freak accident doing a friend a favor. Her tremendous success in her professional life has made balancing her business and personal life even more difficult. But as I said, she is a master here."

The next evening Ray and Carol made the journey to Eleanor Mitchell's house. Carol was feeling a real sense of anticipation.

"I'm excited to meet her," she said.

As they drove up the winding drive to Eleanor's home, the large Tudor house crowning the hill indicated Eleanor's financial success. The sun was beginning to set behind the house, streaking the sky with lavender and brilliant red.

When Eleanor greeted them at the door, her welcome was as gracious as her home was splendid.

After the small talk of getting acquainted, Eleanor began, "I understand from Coach that you are concerned about how to be free so you can align every action with what you really want. Is that correct?"

"Correct!" said Ray. "Seeing myself free in all I do is a tremendous hurdle for me. How I or any person can be truly free in *everything* we do is beyond my comprehension."

"I don't really get it, either," said Carol. "Take today, for example. On a beautiful June day like this one was, I would have loved to play a round of golf. But I had to take the kids to baseball and softball. I didn't feel free to be totally aligned with what I really wanted, which was to play golf."

Ray nodded his agreement. "I was traveling last Wednesday and Thursday, working late and doing those long reports I hate. Sorry, but I just can't see how I was free to be aligned with what I really wanted at that time."

"Great concerns," said Eleanor. "I'm going to ask you to hold those concerns in the back of your minds for about four minutes. Many people—if not most—fail to believe they're free to align all their actions with what they really want. However, to be an Aligned Thinker, you need the insight and attitude to see yourself as free."

Eleanor went to a bookshelf and pulled out a file folder full of cards.

"Look at this diagram," she said, turning over the first card.

"In the freedom insight diagram, P stands for the primary desire," Eleanor explained. "In this example, the primary desire is to be a sports star—football, softball, golf, or any sport. NC stands for necessary condition. NC's are conditions

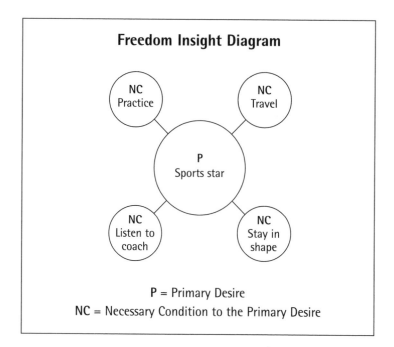

Freedom Insight Diagram

NC
Practice

NC
Travel

P
Sports star

NC
Listen to
coach

NC
Stay in
shape

P = Primary Desire
NC = Necessary Condition to the Primary Desire

that are necessary for achieving what we really want. Necessary conditions are not necessarily wanted in and of themselves. In fact, at times they're a pain. In this sports example, the NCs are travel, stay in shape, listen to the coach, and practice."

"I've never found staying in shape very enjoyable," commented Ray.

"The enjoyment of the NC is not the question," reiterated Eleanor. "Much of our enjoyment depends on our attitude. We might like our coach and practice or not like our coach and practice. All great performers in any field practice regularly and listen to their coaches at some time."

"I still don't see how I'm free to align every action with what I really want," said Ray.

"You will in a minute," said Eleanor. "In the sports example, as in all of life, we have three choices. To use the freedom insight you need to understand your three choices."

Ray and Carol leaned forward and listened intently.

"In choice 1, the P, or the primary desire, is no longer worth the NCs, the necessary conditions. The rational choice is drop or change the P."

"Can you give an example of when you might drop or change the P because of a necessary condition?" asked Carol.

"Sure," said Eleanor. "When you look at history, all sports stars eventually make this rational choice and retire. I know from personal experience there comes a time when there are more important things than being a sports star. So I retired. Some other examples are John Elway, Chris Evert, Wayne Gretzky, Arnold Palmer, and Michael Jordan, to name just a few. Of course, Michael missed the game and made the choice to go back, twice. That's okay, too. Just because you drop your primary desire doesn't mean you can't pick it up again, as long as you're making a rational choice to do so. Each of these dropped being a sports star because the NCs became too much."

"That makes sense. What's the second choice?" asked Ray.

"Choice 2 is to freely choose to become a victim," said Eleanor, "which is an irrational choice. Suppose the potential star says to himself or herself, 'I must practice because the coach said I must! I must stay in shape because the coach said I must!' When the sports star lives by the 'I must' attitude, what kind of effect do you think this has on his or her potential?"

"A negative effect would be my guess," answered Ray. "All that 'I must' stuff would sap the star's energy."

Eleanor nodded. "The sports star would be freely choosing not to be free and would make himself or herself a victim—in this case, a victim of what the coach said. Unfortunately, many people let themselves slip into this victim mentality. It is the 'I must because of so-and-so' attitude."

"So what's the third choice?" asked Carol.

"Choice 3 is to freely choose the NCs to get to the P, a rational choice. In this case, the sports star might say, 'I don't like the coach. But I freely choose to listen to the coach because I want to be a star.' In other words, I accept the necessary conditions—listening to the coach, practicing, staying in shape—not because I like them but because I want the primary desire: becoming a star."

"Can't we just get what we really want—the primary desire—without all the hassle?" asked Carol. "Eleanor, you're the CEO of your own company; you're the boss. Aren't there any Ps that you want that are NC free?"

"I have never come up with one P that doesn't have some NCs connected to it. Some people think a CEO can do it," said Eleanor. "Take one of my purposes—to be a great CEO. Do I have any NCs with this goal?"

Ray answered, "You have clients, employees, and stockholders. You have plenty of NCs as CEO."

Eleanor chimed in, "And you forgot the toughest one: the many government regulations. Carol, let's travel back in time to this morning when you felt like you wanted to play golf but you actually became baseball-softball-taxi mom. Let's say you can do your day over. What are your choices?"

Carol replied, "I could play golf, which I would love to do. Then I could take Tammy to softball and Jamie to baseball."

Eleanor continued, "What did you actually do and why?"

"I gave up the golf and drove the kids," replied Carol.

"Why? What do you value more?" Eleanor asked.

Carol thought for a moment and then replied, "I can play golf when they go off to college. It's important for their growth and maturity that they receive these opportunities now. Golf can wait; their growth can't." She stopped, then added thoughtfully, "You're right, I did what I really wanted this morning. I skipped what I felt like doing. In this case, decision versus a feeling: decision wins. Because I love the kids, I value their opportunities. They were my P."

Eleanor summed up, "So you were totally free to pursue your P, even though you did not necessarily like to give up the golf."

"Right," said Carol, still missing the golf but feeling more enlightened.

"The freedom insight does not say you always like what you choose," said Eleanor. "The freedom insight says you are totally free to choose and make a rational decision related to what you really want. Make sense?"

"When you look at the situation in the light of the freedom insight, it seems like just common sense," Carol responded.

"Ray, does that help you with traveling, working late, and doing reports?" Eleanor asked.

"Yes!" said Ray. "This does give me a completely different outlook on the freedom issue. I'm beginning to see why Coach Eric was so confident when he said you would show us how we are free to align *every action* with what we really want. I believe I understand the freedom insight, but it's going to be a challenge to make the freedom insight my freedom attitude."

"Challenge? Yes. Worth the effort? A huge yes!" Eleanor replied. "In fact, when the freedom insight becomes your freedom attitude, you'll discover you can get rid of interruptions forever."

At the words "get rid of interruptions forever," Ray and Carol were immediately interested and exchanged skeptical glances.

Before they could speak, Eleanor continued, "But that's a challenge for a future day. I want to share with you a card I had on my desk for a long time. If you put this someplace you can see daily and repeat the words regularly, it will help you make this common sense your common practice.

"In a surprisingly short time, this freedom insight card helped me internalize the freedom attitude. Today I feel free with *every action*."

■

My Freedom Insight and Attitude
I choose my P, primary desire;
I accept the NCs, necessary conditions.

CHAPTER TEN

Life Aligning Question Two

THE FOCUS QUESTION

ELEANOR SAID, "I understand from Coach that both of you also feel frustrated because you never get it all done. You're looking for better professional-personal life balance, and you want a method to bridge the gap between what you really want and your here-and-now actions. Is that right?"

"That's right," said Carol. "When we got married, we dreamed about spending a lot of time together. Now that we have two kids, of course, we need to spend time with them. There is always too much to do and we never get it all done. Eleanor, I'm especially interested in hearing a woman's point of view since you are the primary caregiver for your two children and have a career as the CEO of your own business.

"Answering the purpose question—even in writing— was not an immediate solution for me. To go straight from my written life purpose to doing my next most important action seems like an impossible jump. I feel I need something in between. Plus, I get a lot of little to-do's each day. How do I fit those in when I'm supposed to be focusing on my life purpose?"

Responding to Carol's concerns, Eleanor opened her file folder and pulled out another card. "Excellent questions," she said. "This leads us to the Life Aligning Focus Question." She passed the card to Carol and Ray.

The Focus Question
■

*With the many options I have, how do I stay focused on what I **really** want?*

Eleanor continued, "The answer to this question is one of the easiest and most powerful Aligned Thinking tools I know. However, many people don't get the full value because they make one or more of five mistakes. It's sad, too, because each mistake is easy to overcome."

"Five mistakes?" Carol repeated. "I'm afraid to ask what they are because I might have made all five. But I really need to know what they are."

"As I said," Eleanor reiterated, "each mistake is easy to overcome with the Aligned Thinking tools. It begins with a gift to yourself."

"A gift to yourself—what do you mean by that?" asked Ray.

"The gift to yourself is a regular focus period. You have been given 168 hours in a week to do as you choose. To make the other 167 hours richer, more satisfying, and more productive, it seems smart to set aside 1 hour a week for focus periods. This means about fifteen minutes on the weekend and about five minutes at the beginning of each day to focus on where you want to go and to plan the route. Not giving yourself a regular focus period is mistake number one."

"What's mistake number two?" Carol asked.

"Not reviewing your professional and personal life purpose daily," Eleanor replied.

"Why is that?" Ray asked.

"Life Aligning Question Two, the focus question, is, With the many options I have, how do I stay focused on what I really want? The people who are successful in getting what they really want keep this question uppermost in their mind. Remember the definition of the Aligned Thinker? 'What you really want drives every action, and every action takes you back to what you really want.' If you don't review what you really want regularly, it's hard to see how your true purpose will motivate your every action."

"When you put it that way," Ray said, "it seems like more common sense. What's the third mistake?"

"The third common mistake," Eleanor said, "is using a to-do list!"

Taken aback, Carol blurted, "I thought having a to-do list was a good thing."

"I'd be lost without my to-do list," Ray added.

Eleanor smiled and said, "Let me ask you this: When you work hard all day and have more on your to-do list at the end of the day than you had at the beginning, how does that make you feel?"

Ray was quick to answer. "Annoyed! Like I didn't accomplish much." The anguish was clear in his voice. "That's what started me on this journey in the first place. One night on the train home, my life looked as black as the tunnel under the Hudson River outside," Ray summarized his under-the-Hudson frustration.

"Classic to-do list frustration symptoms," Eleanor said. "If you like acronyms, you can call it the TODLIF virus. The 'to-do list frustration virus' is that hopeless feeling you get at the end of the day when you've worked hard for long hours and you go back to your to-do list and discover it's longer than it was at the beginning of the day. You feel like—well, you know what it feels like."

"We sure do," Carol said with a sigh.

"You can get rid of that feeling now—immediately and forever—by using a couple of Aligned Thinking tools," Eleanor said with confidence. "First, you need to distinguish between a to-do list and a priority list with a *holding pen*.

"Using a to-do list to keep track of what needs to be done is better than nothing. Yet nothing can be more frustrating than a to-do list." Eleanor stopped to let them think about that.

"With the to-do list," she continued, "you're working with a contradiction. You want to be creative, and most people are. So as soon as you think of something that needs to be done, you save it on your to-do list. Great! But at the same time, you're hurrying to do all the things listed by the day's end. Thus the contradiction! Add more, and hurry more to get it all done. It's almost impossible to get a sense of completion."

"Exactly, and very frustrating at times," said Ray.

Eleanor continued, "Enter the holding pen, as simple as a pad of paper or as elegant as the most expensive electronic pad. Every time you think of something that needs to be done, put it in the holding pen. During your focus period at the beginning of the day or week, you'll get your priorities for that time from the holding pen, after you review what you *really* want.

"Here's the real difference. You put on your *priority list* only those items *that you can reasonably complete* this day or this week. You plan to make yourself a successful person each day by making a list of priorities that you can accomplish. The way many people plan—especially people who use a to-do list—absolutely ensures they'll have to-do list frustration at day's end."

"Guilty as charged," Carol said with a small smile.

"A lot of this seems to be common sense when you explain it, Eleanor," Ray said, "although I've never thought of it this way before."

"Remember Coach's insight," Eleanor responded. "There's no such thing as common sense, just good sense that is not too common. This is good sense, and it's not too common."

"Yeah," Ray interjected. "I also remember Coach told us our challenge is to implement that uncommon good sense as soon as possible."

"Maybe this will help," Eleanor said. "Let me share one of Coach's stories that made it easier for me to live this not-too-common sense. Consider the story of two committed people who have equal talent and who work equally hard, Mr. To-Do-List Frustration, also known as Mr. Todlif, and Mr. Satisfied.

"At the beginning of the day, Mr. Todlif had thirty things on his to-do list. During the day, he picked up four more. He worked hard all day and even put in an hour extra. At the day's end he checked off the three things he'd accomplished, but he now had thirty-one left to do. As he walked to his car, was he more aware of the three things accomplished or the thirty-one not done?"

"If he's anything like me," said Ray, "he's frustrated about the thirty-one incomplete items."

"That's the way most people answer," said Eleanor. "Yes, Mr. Todlif was frustrated. He was experiencing to-do list frustration. On the other hand, at the beginning of the day,

Mr. Satisfied had a holding pen of thirty things to do. He reviewed the list and selected the three priorities he thought he could complete during the day. As coincidence would have it, he selected the exact same three things Mr. Todlif selected. He put them on his priority list.

"During the day, Mr. Satisfied added four more items to his holding pen. At the day's end, he checked the three things off his priority list. He had accomplished his entire priority list. As he walked to his car, he felt great. It was another day that 100 percent of his priority list had been completed."

Eleanor pulled a card from the file. "This card shows Mr. Todlif's to-do list and Mr. Satisfied's priority list and how they differed at the end of the day. It's pretty obvious who was more satisfied.

"At the bottom, take a look at the formula for satisfaction. Satisfaction does not equal just accomplishment. It equals accomplishment as it relates to your expectations," said Eleanor.

"A very simple step you can take to overcome the TODLIF virus is to create a holding pen and priority list," she continued. "When you determine the few most important things to do for the week or day, put them on the priority list. This gives you a smaller list to focus on. When you do this, you will be controlling your expectations. You set priorities to make yourself a winner each day. The benefit is more satisfaction."

Eleanor passed the card to Carol and Ray.

"I think I get it," said Carol. "If I focus on just my priorities, I'll be more aligned with the important things in my life. By using a holding pen, I'll never lose something, but I won't necessarily be focusing on it today."

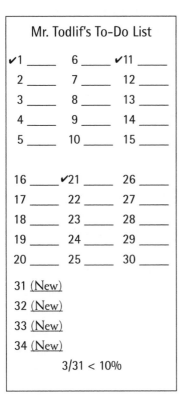

Mr. Todlif's To-Do List

✔1 _____	6 _____	✔11 _____
2 _____	7 _____	12 _____
3 _____	8 _____	13 _____
4 _____	9 _____	14 _____
5 _____	10 _____	15 _____

16 _____	✔21 _____	26 _____
17 _____	22 _____	27 _____
18 _____	23 _____	28 _____
19 _____	24 _____	29 _____
20 _____	25 _____	30 _____

31 (New)
32 (New)
33 (New)
34 (New)

$$3/31 < 10\%$$

Mr. Satisfied's Priority List

✔ 1 _____
✔11 _____
✔21 _____

$$3/3 = 100\%$$

Mr. Satisfied's Holding Pen

	6 _____	
2 _____	7 _____	12 _____
3 _____	8 _____	13 _____
4 _____	9 _____	14 _____
5 _____	10 _____	15 _____

16 _____		26 _____
17 _____	22 _____	27 _____
18 _____	23 _____	28 _____
19 _____	24 _____	29 _____
20 _____	25 _____	30 _____

31 (New)
32 (New)
33 (New)
34 (New)

A Formula for Satisfaction

?

Satisfaction = Accomplishment

$$\text{Satisfaction} = \frac{\text{Accomplishment}}{\text{Expectations}}$$

"Exactly," said Eleanor. "You'll get a triple benefit. You'll achieve more, achieve more of the important things, and feel more satisfied."

"Overcoming to-do list frustration sounds like a dream come true," Ray said with enthusiasm. "The holding pen–priority list is something I want to put into practice immediately."

"You're going to love it," said Eleanor. "All right, let's go on to mistake number four. It's the 'business priorities only virus.' When my husband, Louie, was still living, both of us were totally involved in the business, and we started to drift away from each other. We were on course to create two very successful business careers and one divorce. The simplest of Aligned Thinking tools derailed the divorce train."

Carol nodded. "At times, Ray and I feel like we're drifting apart. So what is this simplest of tools?"

"When you set your priorities for the day or week to come, be sure to include several personal priorities, like time for each other. When Louie and I began to do this, we rebuilt our failing relationship. When our kids came, we scheduled weekly time for each other and with the kids. Now that Louie is gone, it is doubly important I make scheduling time with the kids a priority. As they got older, they needed to schedule time for me. Because we include time for each other, the last few years with the kids have been great ones."

Ray shook his head. "If I really value my wife and kids, which I do, this is just common sense—common sense that I have never used."

"This is certainly a tool Ray and I will use immediately," Carol added.

Eleanor continued, "This brings us to the fifth mistake many—even most—people make. Coach said you two are not only very creative but also very motivated. This means you're probably violating the 'be honest in the morning or frustrated in the evening' principle."

"Uh-oh," said Ray jokingly. "What are we not being honest about?"

"In the morning, be honest about how much you can actually accomplish in one day, or be frustrated at the end of the day when you regularly plan too much and rarely get everything done," Eleanor replied. "I found the best way to admit the truth is to actually guesstimate how long each priority activity will take. When I first began using this principle, I discovered I always overplanned.

"Today, I will still occasionally misjudge a task, but I'm much better. Most of my days—because I go through the process of guesstimating how long each task will take—I complete most of my priorities. I'm a more satisfied person."

The three of them lapsed into a thoughtful silence. The sun was long gone.

"It's getting late," Ray said.

"Before you go," said Eleanor as she handed Ray a card, "take this. It will help you make these tools your common practice on your journey to discover the MIN Secret."

How to Avoid the Five Common Mistakes Related to the Focus Question

1 Give yourself regular weekly and daily focus periods.

2 During your focus period, review your critical items:
   - Your personal and professional missions
   - Items in your holding pen
   - Your schedule for the period to come

3 Use a holding pen and a priority list, not a to-do list.

4 Write your business and personal priorities for the period to come.

5 Guesstimate how long each priority will take and adjust your plans accordingly.

CHAPTER ELEVEN

Living the Freedom Attitude and the Focus Question

THE FOLLOWING Monday morning, Carol gave herself a focus period. She took the last card Eleanor had given them and followed it to the letter. She first put all her to-dos in a new holding pen, a simple pad of paper. Then she reviewed her business and personal purposes and set her business and personal—with emphasis on the personal—priorities for the day to come. When she totaled the amount of time she guesstimated each priority would take, she was stunned.

"Fourteen hours!" she said out loud. "No wonder I'm frequently frustrated at the end of the day. I just plan too much! I can never get it all done!" She thought of Eleanor's "be honest in the morning or frustrated in the evening" principle. With difficulty, she cut her priorities down to seven hours, allowing an hour for the unexpected.

That evening she wore a smile as she drove home. She had accomplished her four priorities. She put her own spin on Eleanor's principle: *being honest in the morning brings satisfaction in the evening.*

Ray's biggest opportunity to live his newly acquired freedom attitude came on Tuesday. One of his associates was having trouble in Chicago. The problem was severe enough that it became necessary for Ray to make an unexpected trip there. When things did not go well, he had to spend the night. In the past he would have been very upset, especially because this last-minute trip had resulted in his missing Tammy's summer league championship softball game. On the flight home, Ray reflected on his new freedom attitude.

I really didn't want this problem, Ray thought. *However, I want an above-average style of living for my family and myself. Solving these types of problems is the NC to my P—the necessary condition to my primary desire—which is an above-average style of living that comes from an above-average income. As I make the freedom insight my freedom attitude, I'm becoming free in every action.* He smiled. *This new freedom gives me a sense of control.*

The following Friday was the beginning of the Independence Day weekend, and Coach had invited Ray and Carol to bring their kids for a good view of the fireworks: his home was on the hill across from the mall. Coach also invited a few of his teenage grandchildren. The young people broke away to picnic high on the hill for an optimal view of the fireworks. The adults opted to stay at the picnic tables with the watermelon.

After the kids were out of earshot, Ray shared with Coach his freedom attitude success. "In the past," Ray said, "I would have been very upset by not being free to see Tammy's game. But as I flew home, focusing on the above-average lifestyle I want gave me a real sense of freedom. Life is taking on more meaning, and my individual actions have greater value."

Carol shared her first experience with guesstimating how much time things would take. "Can you imagine?" she said.

"I planned fourteen hours! No wonder my end-of-the-day feeling was regularly to-do list frustration. The holding pen, my priority list, and guesstimating solved that."

"Tremendous!" Coach, always the cheerleader, smiled proudly.

"But Ray and I still have problems," Carol quickly added, as if to emphasize that they had not arrived yet. "I need help in changing my priorities during the day. I just can't anticipate everything when I set my priorities in the morning. How do I deal with the unexpected and still believe I'm free to align every action with what I really want?"

"I have the same problem," Ray said. "Also, with the freedom insight, I am beginning to see how to align every action with what I really want. But I wonder—am I making every moment count?"

"Great questions," Coach said. "You are asking a form of the now question, which is what you will learn from Woody and Prue Madson, the next couple you meet."

Ray replied, "I want to get to the now question soon. I'm eager to discover the MIN Secret, since you said that's the key that ties all Aligned Thinking together."

"The next couple you meet will explain the now question and help you discover the MIN Secret," Coach replied as the first Roman candle shook the ground and lit up the night sky. "You'll see how it all fits together. Have another piece of watermelon. Let's watch the fireworks."

At that moment, multiple bursts of shimmering red, white, and blue exploded across the night sky. Ray put his arm around Carol and gave her a squeeze.

"This year I feel like I might be celebrating freedom in a whole new way," he said.

CHAPTER TWELVE

Life Aligning Question Three

THE NOW QUESTION

THE FOLLOWING Saturday evening, Carol and Ray met Prue and Woody Madson, who served them a delicious meal of leftovers from a huge party they'd had on Independence Day. After everyone had feasted on beef stroganoff and an excellent cabernet sauvignon, Prue asked, "Did anyone save room for dessert?"

Standing at the head of the table, Prue tempted Ray, Carol, and Woody with a Dutch apple pie. Fresh from the oven, its heavenly aroma filled the room. "It's great with vanilla ice cream," she said with a wicked grin.

Woody and Ray said yes without a second thought. Carol was not so quick to decide.

"I honestly don't know!" She let out an exasperated sigh. "That has to be the most delicious looking pie I've ever seen. But I've been trying to cut down on sugar."

Woody responded, "Your dilemma—what to do this moment—ties right in to the third Life Aligning Question, which starts as a riddle."

Carol and Ray leaned forward slightly in their seats, focusing their full attention on Woody. Something in his tone had sounded rather mysterious, and they were eager to hear what he'd say next.

"Excuse me, Carol," said Prue, "but before Woody tells you the secret of life, was that a yes or a no on the pie?"

"Just a sliver, thank you," Carol replied. "Please hold the ice cream."

"Here is the riddle," said Woody. "What is so precious that you experience it only once, no one else will ever experience it, and you will never experience it again?"

"It sounds like my death," Ray said.

"I was thinking of my birth," Carol said.

"Both are correct," replied Woody. "However, those are only two of the many correct answers. For each of us, our birth is far away. And hopefully our death is also far away. Think of something much closer."

Carol knitted her brow. "Do you mean this moment?" she asked.

"You could mean *each* moment," Ray said. "Each moment is precious. No one ever experienced any of my moments, and I'll never experience any one particular moment again."

"Brilliant!" said Woody with enthusiasm. "The past is gone, and the future is not here yet. So what do you control?"

While he gave Carol and Ray time to reply, Woody reached into a manila envelope and placed a piece of paper on the table. "This illustrates my question," he said. "Our life is like a huge pyramid with a lot of width and height. However, the only thing we control is the point at the top, which is the *now*.

"Your answers are critical," Woody continued, "because if you're going to solve the majority of your problems—like

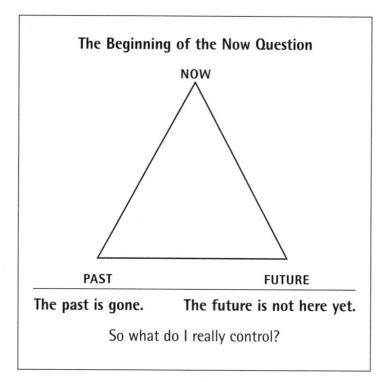

The Beginning of the Now Question

NOW

PAST   FUTURE

The past is gone.   The future is not here yet.

So what do I really control?

frustration, too much to do, not enough accomplishment, lack of professional-personal balance, and not enough meaning in life—you must know where to start. Most people don't make every moment count because they don't know where to start. Knowing exactly what you do and don't control will show you where to start. So, what do you control?"

Ray was the first to answer. "We control what we do in the present."

Carol's face lit up. "This reminds me of the freedom insight Eleanor shared with us. Only I control my actions now. Only I choose to be free and not a victim. It's starting to come together," she said with a smile.

"I think you're ready for Life Aligning Question Three," Woody said as he turned over another card on the table.

The Now Question

∎

*How do I get the most from the only thing I control— my actions **now?***

"How do I get the most from the only thing I control— my actions now?" Carol said, reading from the card. "Good question. I'm not sure I have the answer."

Woody continued, "Some people would say we control both our actions and our attitude now. Since our attitude is one form of our action, we will just focus on controlling our actions now."

Prue came in with plates of pie and ice cream. As she slid a modest sliver of pie in front of Carol, she said, "The big question is, How do I get the most from the only thing I control—my actions now? The question will be easier to answer if we break it into three smaller questions. So let's break this question down into *what*, *why*, and *how*. We'll start with what, as in, What do I want to do now to get the most from this action?"

Ray interrupted eating his pie to make this note:

__What__ do I want to do now to get the most from this action?

"That's not always an easy question to answer," said Carol. "Even when it comes to something as simple as deciding whether or not to have pie."

"Exactly," said Prue. "What to do is not always obvious."

"Let's introduce them to Mr. MIN," said Woody.

Ray frowned. "Does Mr. MIN have something to do with the MIN Secret? Who is Mr. MIN?"

"Mr. MIN," Prue repeated with a smile, "has a lot to do with the MIN Secret. He's a fictional character who will give you some valuable insight about answering the *what to do now* question. But first you have to meet his friends, Mr. Do What I Feel Like and Ms. People Pleaser.

"Mr. Do What I Feel Like was convinced that real freedom meant doing exactly what he felt like," continued Prue. "At first, it meant staying in bed and being late for work. Then it meant quitting work and moving from job to job. These weren't jobs he believed in, by the way—they were just means to an easy paycheck. Because Mr. Do What I Feel Like insisted on his version of freedom, how successful do you think he was in optimizing his inner fulfillment and getting the most from his life?"

"Seems like the guy's functioning on impulse only," said Carol. "His actions seem to be aligned with his feelings." She lifted a forkful of pie and laughed. "Not that I don't have compassion for someone who gives in to impulses! But always doing just what you feel like can lead to disaster."

Prue nodded. "So, doing what you feel like is not a good method for deciding what to do next and making every moment count. Unfortunately, many people use this method—or a variation of it—to live their daily lives."

"What about Ms. People Pleaser?" asked Ray.

"She's well meaning, bless her heart," said Prue. "But she believes that in order to live life right, she should be good to people. So she does what anyone asks. How successful do you think Ms. People Pleaser is in fulfilling her life purpose and goals and making every moment count?"

Ray shrugged. "There is some value in helping others. However, giving up your freedom to the next person you meet is not very smart."

"Well stated," interjected Woody. "Now Mr. MIN, Prue."

"Mr. MIN," Prue said, "sees getting the most from each action as a decision. He figures if he can decide what his Most Important Now—his MIN—is, and does it, he will get the optimal value out of the moment. By definition, there is nothing more important than his MIN."

"His Most Important Now," repeated Ray. "I like that. It's so rational. But how do you decide what your MIN is?"

"We'll get to that," said Woody.

A full moon was rising over the hills beyond Woody and Prue's house. Prue suggested that they refill their coffee cups and move onto the patio to enjoy the warm summer night. As the four of them settled into their deck chairs, a chorus of crickets sang in the field below.

After a few moments, Woody spoke up. "Back to your question, Ray, about deciding what's most important now—your MIN. That's where the why question can help us."

"You mean like, Why do I want to do this now to get the most from this action?" asked Ray.

Ray added Mr. MIN and this question to his notes:

Why do I want to do this now to get the most from this action?

"Yes," said Woody. "And the answer is all about meaning and value. The value of an action comes from the purpose of the action. Here is an important fact: the greatest value for each of us is what we *really* want. That is why it is so important to put what you *really* want from life and work in writing and review it regularly.

"If you want more meaning in your life, create for yourself a bigger life purpose. Coach told us you met Mary and Mike Hall. They're excellent examples of people living a large life purpose. By getting their actions aligned with their life purpose of helping others, they've found great meaning and inner fulfillment. As an Aligned Thinker, what you want from life and work drives every action—in other words, your life purpose—that gives value to your daily activities." Woody paused to give Ray and Carol a chance to let that idea sink in.

"This is reminding me of the Aligned Thinker circle Ed drew on his napkin way back when we were discussing with him and Alanna how to solve our problems," said Carol.

"Ah, yes, the Aligned Thinker circle," Woody said affectionately. "There is a wonderful closed loop here. When what you want from life and work helps you to choose your MIN, your actions will have maximum value. Since this action is chosen because of what you truly value, you have the greatest chance of getting what you truly want from life and work. It's really pretty simple."

Ray said, "If I ask *why* I'm choosing a particular action, I want it to have maximum value. To get maximum value, I go to what I *really* want. So the why of my action that will give me maximum value is related to what I really want. Again, the closed circle. It is elegantly simple, isn't it?"

"Your word "elegant" is appropriate," said Woody. "The dictionary says "elegant" comes from the Latin 'to select.' It has to do with selecting what is richly or tastefully designed. I like to think I select Aligned Thinking as my way of living because it is so rich in design but still so very simple."

Woody continued, "When you discover the MIN Secret, which ties everything together, you will see it is the quintessence of elegance—very rich, extremely simple, and applicable to every moment."

Ray's only thought, expressed with some urgency, was, "Let's push on. I want to discover this MIN Secret as soon as possible."

"First, the *how* question," said Woody. "To get the most from the only thing you control—this moment—you must ask, How do I want to do this action now to get the most from it?"

Again Ray added the question to his notes:

***How* do I want to do this action now to get the most from it?**

"What exactly do you mean by that?" asked Carol.

"I'll explain," said Prue, "with three examples. This time we'll call them Ms. Save Energy, Mr. Many Things, and Ms. In The Flow.

"Ms. Save Energy does things only halfheartedly. She is always saving her energy for later. Ms. Save Energy never puts in a full effort or gives her full attention. How would you see Ms. Save Energy on the one-to-ten inner fulfillment or meaning scale? And where would you put her on the one-to-ten make every moment count scale?" asked Prue.

"I guess if she does things only halfway, she'd be in the fiftieth percentile on both. A pretty low score," said Ray.

"Now let's take Mr. Many Things," said Prue. He believes if he can give 60 percent of his attention to three things at once, he will be 180 percent productive. In reality, he spends 60 percent of his energy running back and forth, so he's actually only 40 percent effective."

"I can relate to Mr. Many Things," Carol said dryly.

"As for Ms. In The Flow," Prue continued, "she organizes every non-MIN item so she can put aside everything except her MIN. This gives her freedom to be totally involved in her MIN with complete focus. She knows where each non-MIN is, so when she needs something, she can retrieve it immediately. But in this moment, she totally abandons every non-MIN item.

"She is aware that she has a limited amount of psychic or mental energy. She also knows that optimal productivity means using all of it on her one MIN. She professes: 'When I'm playing tennis, I want to play tennis. When I sleep, I want to be totally focused on sleeping. When I work, I want to be totally involved in working. In other words, whatever I do, I want to do that one thing totally. I want to always be in the flow.'"

Ray said, "It's pretty obvious that Ms. In The Flow is the person who gets the most out of how to do her next action."

"Exactly," said Woody. "Qualified research has established that if you want an optimal experience, you must be totally involved in what you're doing with all your psychic energy."

For several moments they sat without speaking, at first focusing on the importance of being totally involved in one's MIN. When the focus shifted to the singing of the crickets, Ray got to his feet. "I think the mosquitoes are winning. Do you mind if we escape inside?"

"Let's do it," said Woody.

CHAPTER THIRTEEN

Discovering the MIN Secret

CAROL LOOKED over Ray's shoulder as he sat at Woody and Prue's dining room table writing down the now question. A puzzled look appeared on her face, and it was clear there was a big question coming.

"I hate to say it, but I'm not so sure this is very practical. If I have to stop and think about optimizing the *what*, *why*, and *how* of each action before I decide what to do next, I'll go batty. Isn't there an easier way?"

"Very insightful!" said Woody.

Surprised, Carol and Ray exchanged wondering glances.

"The ability to ask the right question at the right time says you understand," explained Woody. "You asked a very insightful question."

"Thank you," said Carol with a surprised look on her face. "I'm not sure why it is very insightful."

Prue spoke up. "Asking the right question at the right time can empower us or others. Our brain is like a powerful question-answering computer. Each question motivates and guides our powerful computer brain. So you can see how the purpose, focus, and now questions motivate and guide us to take more control of each action and live better lives?"

"Sure," said Carol.

Prue continued, "Your question—'Isn't there an easier way?'—is a very insightful one. It leads directly to the question of questions, the MIN Secret."

"So what is it?" Ray said eagerly.

Woody smiled, "Let's see if you can discover it for yourselves. When you do, you will appreciate it more. The now question asks, How do I get the most from the only thing I control, my actions now? Instead of analyzing the *what, why,* and *how* of your next action, what brief empowering question could you ask to optimize the *what* of the next action?

"I'll give you a hint. It starts with 'what.'"

"How about . . ." Carol hesitated. "This sounds too simple, but how about something like, What's my Most Important Now?"

"Never fear simplicity!" Prue said. "The MIN Secret is simple elegance! You got the first part! 'What's my Most Important Now'—my MIN—captures the *what*." Prue paused a moment to let Ray and Carol assess their progress. Ray added to his notes:

What's my MIN (Most Important Now)?

"Let's move to the *why*," Prue continued. "What brief phrase can you add to get the most meaning or value from your next action?"

Carol thought out loud. "Value and meaning come from what I really want—*my* life purpose. You just emphasized that. So to optimize the *why* of my next action, I could add, 'related to what I really want.'"

"You really are insightful!" said Woody. "You just discovered the MIN Secret. These nine little words, the MIN Secret, will tie everything else together."

"So we come up with, What's my Most Important Now—my MIN—related to what I really want?" said Carol.

With deep satisfaction, Ray added the MIN Secret to his notes:

*What's my MIN, related to what I **really** want?*

"That's the simplicity of it: nine little words," said Woody. "Elegant—rich, simple, and easy to remember as you select what you will do next.

"However, to make the MIN Secret work, you need to be grounded in your answers to the purpose, focus, and now questions. If you don't know what you *really* want or it becomes clouded, it will be hard to answer: What's my MIN, related to a cloud or related to I don't know what?"

"Been there," said Carol with a laugh.

"You also need the freedom insight," Woody continued. "But once you live the answers to the purpose, focus, and now questions and make the freedom insight your freedom attitude so you're free in all you do, you can set all else into the background and just focus on using the MIN Secret.

"That's when the question of questions, the MIN Secret, takes over. You just have to use the MIN Secret when you are starting a new activity. It ties everything else together. When you ask it before each new activity and follow your MIN, you will soon be an Aligned Thinker, enjoying all the benefits."

"Let's go on to the *how*," said Prue. "For that one we ask another empowering question: How can I organize all non-MINs so that I'm free to be totally involved in my MIN with complete focus?"

Ray added this to his notes:

How can I organize all non-MINs so that I'm free to be totally involved in my MIN with complete focus?

"All non-MINs—what does that mean?" Carol asked.

"Once you select your MIN, everything else is your non-MIN. You want to put every non-MIN someplace so you can get it immediately when you want it. But for the time being all non-MINs are out of sight, or at least out of mind." Prue paused, then added, "It's important to remember that as soon as you choose your MIN, you must become totally involved in it with complete focus. Do you have anything to add, Woody?"

"Only to say that asking yourself, What's my MIN? will help you get the most out of every moment, whether you are in the office, with a client, at a ball game, or napping on a Sunday afternoon," said Woody.

"When you are totally involved in your MIN, you will make this moment count. There is no way you can be more productive than being totally involved in your MIN, your Most Important Now. The next time you decide what to do, by using the MIN Secret you will make that moment count. Using the same simple nine-word question, decision after decision, you will eventually make every moment count. You will optimize your life.

This was the payoff Ray had been looking for. He added it to his notes:

When you are consistently totally involved in your MIN, you're making every moment count.

"I'll tell you a personal story about why I love the MIN concept," said Prue. "Early in my career as a professional tennis teacher, life was one big tennis competition. The idea of celebrating life was completely foreign to me. I celebrated only when my tennis students won!

"Then I was introduced to Aligned Thinking. My 'aha' was that I had a great professional life but no personal life. When I wrote what I *really* wanted from life, I dug deep down in my soul and found I wanted to be in love with a wonderful man who loved me in return. My M-I-N was to find an M-A-N!"

The four of them laughed at her play on words.

Prue continued, "It took me a year to find my man and another year to convince him that I was his MIN." Woody and Prue exchanged tender looks. "That was many years ago," she said. "I still teach tennis, but my life is a lot more balanced now. By focusing on my personal MIN, I was able to create a home life that's as rewarding as my career teaching tennis. The MIN concept works for every moment of my life."

Ray and Carol nodded thoughtfully. There was a brief pause.

"Every moment of your life!" Ray repeated slowly. He turned to Carol. "If only I had known about the MIN question in Barbados," he said.

Carol nodded. "I know what you mean."

Responding to Woody's puzzled look, Ray said, "I spent our honeymoon being too stressed out about work to enjoy the idyllic setting and my wonderful new bride. Knowing what I know now—that Carol was my Most Important Now—I wish I could do over our honeymoon in Barbados and set all the non-MINs aside. To paraphrase the poet, the saddest works of tongue or pen are those few words, 'what might have been.'"

Woody replied, "I've been there. When I learned what it means to truly be an Aligned Thinker, there were many days I wished I could live over. The good news is that you have your entire future to enjoy the MIN Secret, one Most Important Now after another.

"That's true," Ray said with a look of relief.

"Any additional questions?" Woody asked.

"Just one," said Ray. "Why is the MIN—Most Important Now—Secret called a secret? When you understand the Most Important Now idea, you just have to admit its powerful elegance. Why call it a secret?"

"Two reasons. First, most people don't understand it, so in some sense the elegance and power of the MIN question is secret to them.

"Second, you have to understand its deeper meaning. If you go to work Monday and just share the nine-word question with someone, they won't get it. You need to experience the answers to the purpose, focus, and now questions and have the freedom attitude to truly understand the MIN Secret and make it work for you.

"Here is a card that will give you a visual summary."

The Key to All Aligned Thinking

■

The MIN (Most Important Now) Secret

*What's my MIN, related to what I **really** want?*

At the start of each new activity,

- Ask, What's my MIN, related to what I *really* want?
- Organize and abandon all non-MINs.
- Become totally involved in your MIN with complete focus.

To get rid of interruptions forever, when new information becomes available, repeat the items above.

Ray, with significant curiosity, immediately asked, "What does it mean, 'to get rid of interruptions forever, when new information becomes available, repeat the items above'?"

"The MIN Secret and the freedom attitude join forces to get rid of interruptions forever," Woody replied.

This made both Ray and Carol very curious. However, before they could ask for more explanation, Woody added, "This is something most people find hard to believe, especially 'get rid of all interruptions forever.' When I first heard it, I strongly doubted it. But this is another thing that is best understood when you experience it for yourself. Coach told me to mention it. But he said he would help you discover it for yourselves."

This had a twofold effect on Ray and Carol. They were disappointed because they wanted to know now. And they could not wait to see Coach.

Since it was getting late, Woody summed up their journey so far. "I congratulate you both. I feel you have a very good handle on 30 to 40 percent of the value of Aligned Thinking."

"What about the other 60 to 70 percent?" asked Carol. "What have we missed?"

"It's one thing to understand the MIN Secret; and that will give you 30 to 40 percent of the value," Woody said with quiet conviction. "There is something about your implementation and your personal experience that our words can't communicate. When you implement the tools yourselves in your unique situations, you'll discover things we can't tell you.

"For example, Coach Eric told us we could get rid of interruptions forever. As I said, I wasn't convinced! However, when I experienced it and realized I could still do justice to my clients, colleagues, and family, it was really a very different 'aha'!"

Prue added, "You haven't yet learned the value of teaching Aligned Thinking to your kids, employees, or salespeople. Or how the tools work to overcome stress in a crisis when you have six things that need to be done yesterday."

"Finally," Woody added, "You don't know how much or how little it will cost to make this common sense your daily, even moment-by-moment practice. The value of your implementing the tools in your own lives is something only you can discover."

"Still," Ray said, "I'm disappointed that in three weeks we have only 30 to 40 percent of the value."

"It's not realistic," Woody replied, "to think in a couple of hours we could share with you all the value we have discovered using the process daily, even hourly, for more than twenty years. However, here is the Aligned Thinking Pyramid Coach gave you three weeks ago. I have filled in an outline of what you have learned. You can see your progress."

Aligned Thinking Pyramid

What's my
MIN,
related to what
I *really* want?

MIN Secret
Most Important Now

Now Question
How do I get the most from the only
thing I control—my actions now?

Focus Question
With the many options I have, how do
I stay focused on what I *really* want?

Purpose Question
What do I *really* want from life and work?

PART TWO

Implementing the MIN Secret in Your Life

CHAPTER FOURTEEN

The Cost of Aligned Thinking

THREE GIFTS OF TIME

THE FOLLOWING evening as they sat around Coach Eric's big oak table, Ray and Carol were filled with questions and emotions. Ray unloaded first.

"I was intrigued by Woody's saying Aligned Thinking could get rid of all interruptions forever. As if that weren't unbelievable enough, he said he could do that and still do justice to his clients, colleagues, and family."

"What Woody and Prue shared was terrific, very positive," Carol jumped in. "When we learned the MIN Secret, it was a high. We saw its elegant simplicity. But it was such a letdown to learn we have a handle on only 30 to 40 percent of the value of Aligned Thinking."

Coach smiled. "I'm glad Woody and Prue did the wonderful job that I was convinced they could do. Look at it this way: Let's say the amount of wisdom you have come away with fills a hundred pages. And let's say you have 99.9 percent of what there is to be learned. How much more value can you expect when you implement the process in your lives?"

With a puzzled look, Carol said, "Very little."

Coach continued, "Now let's go back to the insights that you have gained. Again the total amount of Aligned Thinking wisdom you gained fills one hundred pages, but now you only have 30 percent of what is to be had. How much more wisdom and insight can you expect to get as you implement the entire process?"

Carol smiled and answered, "Neat way to put it. We can expect two hundred or more pages of wisdom and insights. Good!" This satisfied both Ray and Carol. They immediately felt better.

"That's great," Ray said. "What I want to know is, how much is Aligned Thinking going to cost us?"

"Let's find out," Coach responded. "Ray, I'd like you to write on the top of a page, 'Three Simple Gifts to Self.' The first gift involves the purpose question: how long will it take to update your life and work purpose every now and then, once you have it in writing?"

"An hour or two every three months when we have our funday for purpose," Carol replied.

"Now for the second gift," Coach continued. "This involves the focus question: how long will it take you to set weekly and daily priorities?"

Since Ray was busy writing, Carol answered again. "I can do it in fifteen minutes on the weekend and about five minutes each day."

"Ray," Coach said, "when you write that, don't forget Carol's favorite: guesstimating the time needed for each project."

This brought a smile to all as Carol said, "I still can't believe I was setting fourteen hours of work in an eight-hour day. Live and learn."

"The third gift involves the now question and the Most Important Now—MIN—Secret. How long will that take?" Coach asked.

"Five to fifteen seconds when I start a new activity," Ray answered.

"Ray, would you add in your notes, 'when I start a new activity or *when I receive new information.*' You want to get rid of all interruptions, don't you?" Coach added.

"Right! How do I do that?" Ray asked.

"Let's finish the cost of becoming an Aligned Thinker first. Ray, I suggest you take a few minutes now to write up an agreement. When we all agree that you have captured what Aligned Thinking will cost you, we will sign it. Let's also agree to meet each quarter shortly after your funday for purpose for the next year. That will be four times. If that's okay, Ray, write that up and we can sign it."

That was exactly what they did. The agreement looked like this.

Three Simple Gifts to Self

Purpose Question
- 1-2 hours quarterly
- Have funday to update personal and business purposes together
- Take turns planning it, have a meal, and see Coach shortly after it

Focus Question
- 5-15 minutes daily and weekly
- Review business and personal purpose
- Set daily and weekly personal and business priorities for the period to come
- Keep all the nonpriorities in the holding pen
- Guesstimate the time needed and adjust priorities

Now Question and MIN Secret
- 5-15 seconds at the start of each new activity or when I receive new information
- Ask, What's my MIN, related to what I really want?
- Organize and abandon all non-MINs
- Be totally involved in my MIN with complete focus

Agreed

Carol Walters   *Ray Walters*   *Coach Eric*

CHAPTER FIFTEEN

Get Rid of Interruptions Forever

NOW THAT gives me a feeling of accomplishment," Ray said as he handed Coach the signed agreement. "This is a milestone."

Coach smiled at Ray and said, "So Woody said that you can get rid of interruptions forever. When I first started in the business, I couldn't believe that either. But I do today.

"Let me help you understand the one-two punch that is the key to this. Of all the interruptions you get, Ray, which annoys you the most?"

The question took no time for Ray to answer. "When my boss calls and says, 'Ray, I have a problem. Can you come over for just a minute?' That 'just a minute' can take many hours. It happens about once a month."

"Great example," Coach commented. "For the moment, I want you to forget you ever heard of Aligned Thinking. Suppose Monday is an important day. You go in early. By nine o'clock you would probably have the first thing done and be moving on to the second.

"Now the phone rings and your boss says those famous words—"

"'Infamous' would be better," Ray interjected.

"Okay, those infamous words. Your boss says, 'Ray, I have a problem. Can you come over for just a minute?' Of course you go. But how much is your heart really in it?"

"Not much," replied Ray. "About 70 percent of me would be going over to the boss. The other 30 percent would still be back wanting to work on the priorities I set in the morning."

Coach asked, "Do you think this hurts what you do for your boss?"

"Absolutely," Ray said with a frown. "It annoys me that he doesn't just say 'This is an important deal and I need you the rest of the day.'"

"In this case," Coach continued, "it does not take till five. It takes till six and the kids are playing ball tonight. You'll miss more than half their games. When you go back to your to-do list, what might you write?"

"I probably wouldn't write anything but would be running for the train. Later I might write on the to-do list, 'Forget it! Nothing has changed with this boss.'"

"So, Ray, how does this make you feel?" Coach asked.

Ray thought a minute. "Angry, frankly. Meanwhile, my boss is happy. He got his problem solved."

"So what would you give to not be angry? What would you give to get rid of interruptions forever?" Coach asked.

"A lot, because I don't like to be angry. It's hard to work that way. Besides, getting rid of interruptions would be terrific," Ray emphasized.

"So here is all it will cost," said Coach. "First, when you get what many call an interruption, stop and think, *This is new information*." Coach paused to let that sink in. "Got it?"

Ray nodded. "I think so. When I have an interruption, I pause and think, *This is new information.*"

"Perfect!" said Coach. "Not everyone is willing to do that, but it's a very powerful insight. Second, you apply the freedom insight: 'I choose my P, primary desire; I accept the NC, necessary condition.' This is the one-two punch.

"If you apply this technique, I can guarantee you'll have success stories when you come back in three months, after your first funday for purpose," Coach concluded.

Ray was willing but more than a little unsure of the outcome.

Ray did not have to wait long to receive his first call from his boss. On Thursday, Ray went in to work thirty minutes early because both his children had games that afternoon. On the way in, he reviewed his professional and personal missions. He took the priorities from his holding pen, guesstimated the time needed, and made the appropriate adaptations. When he arrived at work, he hit the ground running.

He had checked off the first priority and was working on priority number two when, just as he'd predicted, his boss called and said, "Ray, I have a problem. Can you come over for a minute?"

Ray hung up the phone, and following Coach's advice, stopped to review the one-two punch. *This is new information,* he thought. He remembered Woody's advice:

To get rid of interruptions forever, when new information becomes available, ask,

*What's my Most Important Now— MIN—related to what I **really** want?*

What do I really *want?* Ray asked himself. He quickly reviewed the freedom insight he was working to make his freedom attitude.

Accept the NC (necessary condition)
to get my P (primary desire)

What do I really *want from work; what's my P?* Ray asked himself. *I want an above-average lifestyle for the family I love,* he reminded himself. *That means I need an above-average income. My NC is helping the boss solve his problem. Solving the boss's problem is a step closer to the raise I need. This is really an opportunity. My boss's problem is my MIN, my Most Important Now!*

To help himself shift his mental focus completely toward his boss, on his priority list next to the priority he was setting aside, he wrote, "Boss's problem is my opportunity."

When Ray arrived at the boss's office, he was 110 percent committed because he saw this moment as a great opportunity. As in Coach's scenario, he finished work at 6:00 p.m. that evening. He stopped by his office before leaving for the night. Unlike in Coach's version, he was full of hope. Most important, he had done what he *really* wanted. His MIN was moving to his P. This gave him meaning. He recalled what Mike told him three weeks ago: "Activities that give life meaning also give 'here and now' energy."

He moved the priorities he hadn't completed to the next day and wrote, "110 percent focused on what I *really* wanted all day."

While he regretted that he would get to his children's games late, he saw the children, Carol, and himself getting something significant out of this opportunity. His boss would not forget Ray's 110 percent focus and commitment to solving his problem.

Similar situations came up periodically in the following weeks. Occasionally the new information came from the boss. It also came from clients, peers, and direct reports. Ray began to make the one-two punch his daily habit and didn't have to spend as much time stopping and thinking. He learned to deal with new information for what it really was—new information.

Ray had paid the price, and he thought it was a small one, considering his return on investment. Because he was willing to accept a new way to look at new information, interruptions were a thing of Ray's past.

The freedom attitude was adding to Ray's peace of mind and to his control over his life and work.

CHAPTER SIXTEEN

Why It's Dangerous to Teach Aligned Thinking to Kids

AS THE summer continued, Ray and Carol daily discovered more ways the MIN Secret and the Aligned Thinking tools helped them enjoy their ideal professional and personal lives. One day as they were celebrating the moment with iced tea by the pool, Ray said, "I think it's time we take up Woody's challenge to share the tools with the kids."

"A worthwhile challenge," said Carol. "We need some kind of opportunity. Something to motivate them. Got any ideas?"

Ray and Carol had sipped their iced tea thoughtfully for a few moments when Jamie and Tammy appeared. From the looks on their faces, it was obvious they wanted something.

Tammy began. "It's my turn to plan family night. We want one more family day before Jamie goes off to college in three weeks."

Then it was the college freshman-to-be's turn. "You know how you always say we should take responsibility for being creative? So Tammy and I have researched the possibilities.

Six Flags Great Adventure has a special: bring three, get the fourth free."

Ray nearly said no without thinking. The family's entertainment budget was already depleted for the summer. And with Jamie going to college, funds were tight. However, Ray caught Carol's eye. This was the opportunity they were looking for.

"We congratulate you on the research. Give Mom and me five minutes," he said.

After a huddle with Carol, Ray offered this bargain to Jamie and Tammy: "We'll squeeze the budget and go in two weeks if you two will agree to give us your undivided attention for one hour before we go and for two hours driving there."

"To do what?" Jamie asked.

Carol responded, "We want to share the Aligned Thinking tools and MIN Secret. It will help you in school to get what you *really* want."

Tammy and Jamie caucused. They had noticed changes in their parents and wondered why. They were curious about this MIN Secret. Jamie said, "It's a deal. We'll give you the three hours' focus. But you can't bug us after that."

So it was agreed. Two nights before the outing, Ray and Carol walked Tammy and Jamie through Life Aligning Question One: the purpose question. They were able to do it in a half hour. They spent the last half hour working with the kids on what they *really* want from life and work, which was school for them.

As he was working through the purpose question with his dad, Jamie said, "All I can think I really want now is a girlfriend."

Ray replied with a smile, "That's not a bad start. Let's think ahead. Suppose you find that great girl, like I found Mom. What would you need to do to keep her in your life?" That got Jamie thinking about his future. Ray adapted the process Mary and Mike had shared with him to Jamie's situation.

On the way to the amusement park, Carol, sitting in the back seat with Tammy beside her and Jamie in the front seat, walked them through the rest of the Aligned Thinking tools and the MIN Secret.

As the teenagers rode the roller coaster for the fifth time that afternoon, Ray and Carol got another iced tea and found shade. Ray asked, "How do you think sharing the Aligned Thinking tools went?"

"I'm not sure. Like they promised, we got their full attention. They asked good, challenging questions. What results can we expect? Jury's out."

Driving home after this wonderful day filled with sun and excitement, the family had a clear MIN, a Most Important Now, that they were totally involved in with complete focus. Ray's MIN was to drive safely. Carol, Tammy, and Jamie's MIN was to sleep.

After supper the next night, Carol brought out a platter of freshly baked chocolate chip cookies. As they helped themselves to seconds, Ray and Carol joked about their waistlines. Tammy used the occasion to erase any doubt that she understood the MIN concept all too well.

"Dad," said Tammy, "why don't you stop complaining about your waistline and set a goal? Each morning, get up twenty minutes earlier and jog. And when you're in bed don't ask, Do I want to get up? When it's 5:45 a.m. you should ask, What's my MIN, aligned to that fifteen pounds I want to lose? That ought to make you get up."

Carol laughed so hard she started to choke on her cookie.

"I wouldn't laugh so hard, Mom," Jamie continued the chide. "Weren't you telling us you wanted to lose twenty-five pounds? When you're taking that fourth cookie, don't ask, What do I want? That's a bad question. You're supposed to ask, What's my MIN, aligned with what I *really* want? You'd look so much better if you aligned your MIN to losing that extra weight."

Ray looked at Carol and smiled. "We're busted, honey. Isn't there a quote from the Bible that says, 'Out of the mouths of babes'?"

"I didn't mean to preach at you," said Tammy.

"That's okay," said Carol as she turned to her daughter. "You're right, of course. I didn't realize teaching you the MIN Secret would be so dangerous!"

CHAPTER SEVENTEEN

Overcoming Stress in a Huge Crisis

THE FIRST funday for purpose in September was Ray's treat. He found a wonderful restaurant on the east side of the Hudson overlooking the Tappan Zee Bridge. After he and Carol reviewed and refined their purpose for working and living, they enjoyed a delicious meal while watching the sunset across the river, which at that point in time was a three-mile red sea.

"If every day were as peaceful as this one," Carol said as she gazed at the setting sun across the water, "it would be easy to fulfill my new goal of reducing stress at work and at home."

"You work on reducing stress and keeping your blood pressure down, and I'll work on my new goal of serving our community," said Ray.

As summer turned to fall, Ray took a big step toward fulfilling his goal by running for his town's board of finance. Just a month before the elections, his business sent him to China.

During an overseas phone call he asked Carol, "How's it going?"

"It's a little tight," she said candidly. "I've made big strides at work, but as a result I have a lot of new responsibilities. Without you here I have to make sure that Tammy gets where she needs to go for field hockey and all her other activities. Keeping in touch with Jamie is a new challenge. In the evenings, I'm chief taxi driver. During the day, I'm chief transportation coordinator. Plus, I'm working on getting your campaign material out. Thankfully, I've learned to let the things in my holding pen just sit there."

"Keep up the good work," said Ray. "I really miss you and the kids. But as you know, I'm doing my MIN aligned with what I really want—creating an above-average lifestyle for us."

A week later Carol woke to storm clouds and strong winds. She'd planned to get Ray's campaign literature into the mail that day, but by noon the winds had turned to gales and the rain was coming down in torrents. It was very rare for hurricanes to come as far north as their town, but by afternoon, hurricane warnings were being broadcast on every channel.

I'm not going to view this hurricane as an interruption, thought Carol, *I'm going to see it as an opportunity.* She took the time at home to catch up on some work from her briefcase. It took two full days for the weather to clear. By that time Carol was behind on sending out Ray's campaign flyers.

What actions could I take to make up for lost time? Carol asked herself. With just two weeks until the elections, she gathered a group of friends together to help stuff campaign envelopes.

As they stuffed and chatted, Jamie, home for the weekend, popped his head into the den. "Mom, it's for you," he called in a routine manner.

But the phone call was not routine. Carol listened in shocked silence as she learned that Ray's mother had just passed away. Ray was an only child. Her thoughts instantly went to her husband in China.

For the next few minutes, Carol's thoughts raced and her blood pressure shot up. *I need to call the family,* she thought. *I need to find Ray. What about the funeral? I need to let my people at work know I have an emergency. What about Ray's campaign? I need to cancel some meetings.*

She felt herself going into a tizzy and suddenly recognized that she'd been hit by the fear that she could never get done all that she needed to do. She remembered Coach saying that being motivated to do too many things at once is a frequent cause of stress. Carol took a deep breath and thought, *What's my MIN, related to what I really want?*

She took a piece of paper and made a holding pen list. Then she selected her MIN, Most Important Now. She knew that the first thing she wanted was to find Ray. For the moment everything else was a non-MIN. As she focused on finding Ray, she could feel her blood pressure coming down.

It was four in the morning in China. She could do nothing about that for four hours. She took the rest of her list and added names of friends that she would ask to help. Some of the friends who were helping stuff Ray's campaign literature agreed to take items from her holding pen.

She delegated the campaign work to one friend. She delegated the funeral arrangements to another friend, instructing that they be delayed until Ray got home. With each action, she felt herself growing calmer.

It took twenty-four hours to locate Ray and two days to get him home. Carol had to grieve the loss of a wonderful mother-in-law as well as support Ray in his grief. Again and again she used the MIN Secret, "What's my MIN, related to what I really want?"

She reviewed her holding pen list frequently, refusing to let her priority list get too long. She continued to stay focused on her MIN. Jamie stepped up to be the taxi driver for his sister. Even Tammy helped, dropping the "heated discussions" with her brother. Channeling her stress into action, Carol moved from MIN to MIN, focusing all her energy on one thing at a time.

Two weeks later, the crisis was behind them. Ray was elected to the board of finance, and he and Carol spent the evening celebrating with friends at a postelection party. After the last guest headed home, Ray put his arm around his wife. Carol responded with a kiss.

"You're a winner," she said.

"Thanks to you. I don't know how you pulled all this off," he said appreciatively. "You had to deal with a hurricane, Mom's death, finding me in China, getting me home, and the election. How did you do it without a major stress attack?"

"I applied everything we learned from Coach Eric," Carol replied. "The bottom line is I could only do one thing at a time. The MIN Secret was the critical key. Once I made a list of things to do and asked, What's my MIN? I realized I'd have to get help with the rest. Fortunately, we have great friends and kids who picked up the non-MIN duties. Finding you was my first MIN. When I did that, I went to my next MIN. I focused all my mental and psychic energy on my MIN. I didn't allow any extra mental energy to let the stress build up. I'm not going to say that it was perfectly stress free. Losing your mother while you were away in China was definitely stressful. But I didn't allow the stress to take over. My MIN and I were in control!"

"Congratulations," said Ray, "I think you're the real winner tonight."

CHAPTER EIGHTEEN

How to Develop More Motivated, Satisfied Employees

MOTIVATION! The Production Department new hires lack it!"

Ray could tell by Ted Roland's frustrated tone that he was upset. Ray just didn't know why Ted had come to his office to discuss the matter. Ted was the director of human resources—not Ray's area. What did new hires have to do with him? Ray's question was soon answered.

"Your department is amazing, Ray," declared Ted. "At the last company meeting, the president commended you for being under budget and ahead of schedule on your last three projects. Yet a lot of your people are new. How do you do it? More to the point, how do you get your people to do it? Can you tell me what you do in a few words?"

"Let me ask you a question," Ray responded. If you couldn't see the things you do at work leading to what you really want, would you be motivated?"

"No, of course not!" Ted said with some emphasis.

Ray continued, "On the other hand, if you saw everything you did at work as steps toward getting what you really want, would you be motivated?"

"Absolutely! But how does this connect to motivating my new hires?" Ted asked.

"When your people see that what they do every day aligns with what they really want, motivation comes naturally."

"And how do you get them to see that connection?" was Ted's immediate comeback.

"The trick is guiding them to discover it for themselves," Ray replied.

"You sound confident that you could do that. Would you help me put together a training day for the new hires in the Production Department?"

Ray agreed. He and Ted designed the training, and Ray agreed to lead it.

A week later Ray stood before a roomful of new faces. "Welcome," he said. "I'm going to start today by asking everyone to write the answer to the following question." Ray wrote in large letters on a presentation board:

Question One:
What do you really want from work?

Ray's question was met with silence. A few people exchanged questioning looks.

"Let me help you a little," said Ray as he put a Power-Point presentation onto the screen. "Here is a list of possibilities to get you started."

Ray paused to let the possibilities sink in. Income, skills, training, and camaraderie—the list covered the entire screen.

"Think about it," Ray continued, "What do you really want from working here? When you write the answer to this question, it will help you get more of what you really want. When you can see by your actions here at work that you're getting what you really want by being here, it will help you stay focused and motivated. Your work will have more meaning for you. Please jot down your thoughts."

When it appeared that everyone had stopped writing, Ray continued, "Here's question two." Again he wrote in large letters:

Question Two:
Who are your significant others, and what do you want to give them from your work?

As before, Ray paused to let people think. He knew these were two motivating questions because they related directly to each individual and the people closest to them. If he could get this group to align what they really wanted with what they were doing in their jobs every day, he could inspire good performance. It was really just a matter of enlightened self-interest.

"And now for question three," said Ray as he wrote:

Question Three:
What will you give to your customers— those you serve—to earn what you want from work?

"Your customers can be internal, external, or both. In any case, they're the people you serve. Take your time answering this one," Ray said.

After several minutes, Ray spoke again. "And finally, question four."

Question Four:

What will you give to this company to earn what you want from work?

Ray concluded, "You have just created a purpose for working that aligns what you want from your company with what you will give to earn it. You now have your own individual mission for working."

After a short break Ray taught the new hires the freedom insight. He also taught them the focus question and the powerful concept of the Most Important Now. By the end of the day he helped them discover the MIN Secret. When the new hires began joking about living their MIN, Ray knew this was a sign that they were really getting the idea.

After joining in the fun, Ray pointed out that the last part of the MIN Secret, "related to what I really want," took the new hires back to their mission for working that they had created first thing in the morning.

"You now have the power to create a quadruple win," he told them, "for your significant others, those you serve, your company, and most of all, for yourselves."

The improved performance in the Production Department was noticeable almost immediately. When the next production report came out, Ted Roland came to see Ray again. "I want to thank you for what you did for the new hires."

For Ray, the best gauge of his success was what Ted said just before he left. "Most of all, I want to thank you for what you did for me. The MIN Secret helps me many times daily. A month ago I came asking for help to motivate the new hires. Today I come back feeling more motivated and satisfied myself because now I can see how my Most Important Now relates to what I *really* want."

CHAPTER NINETEEN

How to Help Salespeople Sell More

RAY WASN'T the only one who had success bringing the Aligned Thinking tools into the workplace. On a rainy morning in October, Chuck Bonner, vice president of world-wide sales, telephoned Carol for an impromptu meeting.

Walking to his office, she felt a touch of nervousness. What did he want from her? Chuck had a reputation for being a very tough boss. He had publicly opposed the company-wide learning program Carol had recently sponsored. She knew from experience that he could be difficult to deal with. If an idea did not contribute quickly to the bottom line, he would be against it. He did get results. Hesitantly, she knocked on his door.

Without so much as a greeting, Chuck got right to the point. "I just received the results of a two-year study," he said. "Our research shows that the more time our salespeople spend with our customers, the more they sell. Can you find a program that will get our people to organize their time so they spend maximum hours with the customers? This is especially important for our experienced salespeople. They're the ones who sell the most."

Carol nodded. "Yes, I—"

"It can't be an ordinary time management program," Chuck said, cutting her off, "because all our senior people have been through those programs. It's got to be something new, quick to understand, easy to use. And it has to give them something to help them personally, or they won't use it."

Chuck was not in a mood to be crossed. He kept his job as vice president of worldwide sales because he produced results. Solving this problem for him would enhance Carol's reputation as chief learning officer. Just as important, the sales staff would be empowered and the whole company would benefit.

"Tell me more about what you need," she said.

"Whatever program you find has to be a process. Our experienced salespeople are all engineers, and engineers love a process. The process has to be repeatable. I want to teach it once and benefit from it for twenty to thirty years. The benefits need to be immediate and they need to last a lifetime!"

"I think I have just the program," Carol said.

"Is that right?" Skeptically, Chuck lifted a brow.

"It's called Aligned Thinking." Carol gave him a brief overview of the results he could expect, telling him only enough to make him curious.

"Is this program expensive?" Chuck asked.

"When you consider the return on investment you're looking for, it's a bargain," Carol replied. "And if we're lucky, I'll be bringing in an expert."

On a cold but sunny December afternoon, Carol leaned against one of the majestic stone lions outside the New York City Public Library. It was her turn to be in charge of the funday for purpose. Ray walked up the steps at the agreed-upon time of 3:00 p.m.

They found a quiet place inside to review the last quarter. Together they brainstormed new ideas about their life purpose and goals. It seemed that the more they shared Aligned Thinking with their children, friends, and employers, the more value they discovered. By the time they were done, it was past five o'clock.

"We've got to go," said Carol. "Our reservation is at five-thirty." To Ray's delight, Carol had arranged for dinner at their favorite midtown restaurant and, somehow, tickets to the hottest show on Broadway.

"It was outstanding," Ray conceded to Coach after their funday for purpose meeting later that month. "We had front-row-center seats. I must admit, that play beat my dinner with the sunset over the Hudson."

"I'm glad you guys are making funday for purpose a celebration, because that's what it's supposed to be," said Coach.

"I've got a lot to celebrate this quarter, thanks to you," said Carol. "You did such an outstanding job training our sales force that Chuck Bonner had a dozen roses delivered to me with a note that said, 'To my hero: 90 percent of the participants say the process will help them spend more time in front of customers; 92 percent say they believe they will be more satisfied at the end of the day.' Coach, thanks for making me a hero!"

"Thanks for the business," said Coach. "I'm glad it went okay."

"Better than okay!" exclaimed Carol. "Chuck plans to send me to our Beijing headquarters to find out if Aligned Thinking will work with our Asian sales force. I never in my wildest dreams thought that would happen! Chuck Bonner is not an easy man to please."

Coach nodded. "He has a very tough job. The VP of worldwide sales has to keep a lot of people happy—clients, salespeople, management. He was demanding. So are a lot of VPs and CEOs. My partners and I did for him what we'd do for anyone. Congratulations on the Asia trip."

"The MIN Secret takes me to Asia. Wow!" announced Carol.

Coach smiled. "Do you see what Woody meant when he said after three weeks you probably only had a handle on 30 to 40 percent of the value of the MIN Secret and the Aligned Thinking tools?"

Ray replied, "Probably he should have said 10 to 20 percent. That would have been more accurate. But I'm glad he didn't. Saying 30 percent scared us enough."

Carol was quick to agree. "I had no idea how much could change from such a simple nine-word question. And it's so low maintenance. Just the gift of the three focus periods. That's all it costs."

"As you continue to implement these tools, there is much more to come," Coach added. "But I want the big report— how are your weight loss and jogging goals coming along?"

Ray smiled and jumped in. "I taught Tammy what gets measured gets done. Careful what you teach your kids! When I was having trouble jogging and losing my fifteen pounds, Tammy set up a record-keeping system for me and encouraged me to ask, What's my MIN, related to those ugly fifteen pounds? when 5:45 a.m. rolled around. According to

Tammy, I have an 80 percent jogging record and have lost seven pounds."

Carol added, "And I've lost ten pounds. Every time I go for a second helping or another cookie, Coach Tammy encourages me to ask, What's my MIN, aligned to the twenty-five pounds I want to lose? This Aligned Thinking stuff in the wrong hands is dangerous."

The three of them laughed.

"Congratulations on raising such smart kids," said Coach. "Of course, I think I know where they got their brains."

CHAPTER TWENTY

Are You Living Your Ideal Professional and Personal Life?

RAY HAD really outdone himself with the last funday for purpose: a surprise ski weekend in Vermont. Tammy and Jamie had skied until the lifts closed, while Ray and Carol quit early on Saturday to review their life and work purposes. With his son and daughter's help, Ray had pulled the trip off as a total surprise. Carol, a fierce competitor, had promised to top it this quarter.

Since this was June and the one-year anniversary of their beginning the Aligned Thinking journey—a journey that had turned into a pilgrimage to fulfill their life's purpose— Ray suspected something big was coming. It was the planner's privilege to assign the surprised any reasonable task in preparation. A month ago, Carol had asked Ray to take this Thursday through Monday off. Last night, she had handed him a sealed envelope that read, "Do not open till you are on the train going to work."

As the train rumbled through the tunnel, Ray opened the note. It read:

Dear Ray:
Are you living your ideal professional and
personal life today? If so, what does it cost?

Inside the note was the list of professional and personal life ideals they had given Coach a year before.

Our Ideal Professional and Personal Life

We hope becoming Aligned Thinkers will help us

1 Overcome the frustration of too much to do

2 Increase accomplishment and satisfaction

3 Reduce stress

4 Increase quality personal and family time

5 Enhance meaning and happiness

6 Make every moment count so life becomes
  a celebration

Ray smiled. "Okay, boss," he said under his breath. *I can check number one on our list, "Overcome the frustration of too much to do,"* he thought. In the past he had assured his own frustration by planning too much. But he'd learned from Eleanor's wisdom: "In the morning, be honest about how much you can actually accomplish in one day, or be frustrated at the end of the day." He checked off number one with genuine satisfaction.

I can definitely check number four, "Increase quality personal and family time," Ray thought. Since instituting the funday for purpose and Wednesday family nights some time ago, Ray and Carol really did have quality time together and with their kids.

Everyone took turns planning the activities. More often than not it was an evening of fun card games, which Ray enjoyed.

At the office later that morning, a meeting broke up early and Ray found he had fifteen extra minutes before his regular Wednesday lunch with friends. A temporary employee named Julie was taking his executive assistant's place that day. As he walked by her desk, he noticed she was crying. With fifteen minutes to spare, he asked her if she wanted to talk.

"No, it's okay," she said, averting her eyes.

But Ray could tell she needed a friend. "You sure?" he asked.

She hedged. "Well . . ."

"Come on into my office," Ray said.

Ray studied the shy, capable Julie as she took a seat.

"I'm sorry to trouble you, Mr. Walters. This has been a very tough month for me. My engagement of six months broke up two weeks ago. This week I found out my mother has cancer. My father died when I was fourteen, and I'm an only child."

"I'm sorry to hear that," Ray said. He offered her a tissue.

"Excuse me for falling apart," she said, reaching for the tissue.

"It's okay, we all have bad days."

As Julie wiped her tears, Ray did some quick thinking. This was shaping up to be a situation requiring more than fifteen minutes. *What's my MIN?* he asked himself. If this were his boss calling, the answer would be easy. This would be an opportunity to move closer to that above-average income for that above-average lifestyle. If this were a client, the answer would be easy as well. But this was a temporary helper on her last day.

The old Ray would have seen this as an interruption to his lunch. But for the new Ray there were no interruptions, only new information. *What's my MIN?* he repeated to himself.

Ray did not want to miss lunch with the boys. But Julie needed someone to talk to now, not later. To take time with her after work would mean coming home late on a family night—not an option. Ray asked the question a third time, this time using all nine words:

What's my MIN, related to
*what I **really** want?*

Before he answered, Ray thought of the empowering question he'd asked during his focus period that morning:

What opportunities, planned and unexpected,
will I have today that will move me closer to
fulfilling my life purpose and goals?

Isn't one of my primary purposes to help others, starting with the family but including friends and employees? he asked himself. At that point Ray knew what to do.

"Would you like to go to lunch?" he asked.

"Really?" Julie looked at him hopefully. "That would be great."

While she was getting her purse, Ray called one of the boys and explained the situation. He was committed to supporting Julie in her time of need. By two o'clock, he understood her situation. When he returned from lunch, Ray helped Julie get an appointment with a counselor. He also found another department in the company in need of temporary help and arranged for her employment to be extended.

Ray was now running thirty minutes behind schedule. Even so, he went back to his ideal professional and personal life list and checked number three, "Reduce stress." Ray had found at lunch—and many times in the past few months— that when he was totally involved in his MIN with complete focus, he had no psychic energy left to be stressed about nonpriorities. These days Ray perceived no stressful interruptions, only new information and opportunities.

Ray added a check at the bottom. If there were a number seven, it would have been "Decrease interruptions." When he wrote his ideal professional and personal life list, decreasing interruptions had been too much to even dream about.

Ray returned to his priority list. One of today's priorities was the monthly report, the thing that Ray used to hate the most. The old Ray would procrastinate—get a soft drink and put it off. He understood why Tammy often said, "Suppose I don't feel like doing it?" In the past, Ray was frequently a victim of selecting his next activity aligned to what he felt like.

The new Ray asked, *What's my MIN, related to what I really want?* Ray knew the dreaded report was next. Now he had a higher goal. Not only did he want to feel the accomplishment and satisfaction of completing the report, he also wanted to celebrate life as he was doing it.

He had his own technique. First, he would not permit himself to fret about being a half hour behind schedule. That would sap precious psychic energy and generate stress. On a small piece of paper he wrote, "2:00 to 2:30 p.m. first quarter of the report—then a soda reward."

He knew he wanted to celebrate this moment, his freedom and his ability to be totally aligned to what he wanted. *What I really want is an above-average style of living for my wonderful family. One of the keys is to produce well-written monthly reports.*

That's my MIN. He did not want to focus on the entire report. Two hours seemed like too much to conquer. Thirty minutes with a soda reward—he could handle that. Seconds later, Ray was totally involved in the report with complete focus, forgetting that he hated it.

To his surprise, it was three o'clock before he thought of the soda. By then he was halfway done. The dreaded report wasn't so dreadful because he was able to become totally involved with complete focus.

Forget the soda, he mused. *I'll just push on and finish.* A little after three thirty, he was done. The report was a triple victory: First, he had celebrated his life and freedom by being totally involved in what he really wanted, an important step to his above-average income and lifestyle. Second, the hated report was not so bad. Third, he went home with far more energy than he would have dreamed possible a year ago.

After settling into his seat for the train ride home, Ray scanned the *New York Times.* When the train entered the tunnel under the Hudson, he put down the paper and reflected. A year ago, his life had seemed as black as the tunnel outside the window.

Too much to do!
So little control over my life!
Life doesn't seem to have much meaning anymore.

How clearly he recalled that day. He shook his head and thought about what being aligned to what he really wanted— the mark of the Aligned Thinker—had done for his life.

I can honestly say that I am creating my life and work as I want them to be, he thought. *I can definitely check number five,*

"*Enhance meaning and happiness.*" He smiled as his thoughts turned to what he had done for Julie.

In the past, he would have considered himself a hero, helping another human being. This evening he considered himself blessed to have been of service. This felt so much more meaningful than being a hero.

Again he reviewed the dream list that he and Carol had first presented to Coach Eric. He remembered his hesitancy in giving Coach the list, afraid they were asking for too much. He thought about the second item on the list, "Increase accomplishment and satisfaction." *Today I'm accomplishing much more, especially of the important things,* Ray thought.

And satisfaction? He remembered a year ago, when his life had looked blacker than the tunnel outside. When he'd talked to Coach Eric, it seemed there might be light at the end of the tunnel. Ray looked away from the blackness outside the window and into the brightly lit car of the train. *This brightness is a symbol of my present life. Yes, Carol, to answer the first question in your note, I am living my ideal professional and personal life,* he thought.

Just then the train emerged from the tunnel and sunlight burst through the windows, making the previously bright interior pale by comparison. *This is my life!* Ray thought. *Better than our dream life come true. How perfect the timing!* He checked off number two, "Increase accomplishment and satisfaction." Finally, he checked off number six, "Make every moment count so life becomes a celebration."

He could hardly wait to get home and find out what surprises his wonderful, competitive wife had in store to top his funday for purpose Vermont ski weekend. What a difference a year had made.

CHAPTER TWENTY-ONE

A Brilliant Future

HI, EVERYBODY," Ray greeted his family with enthusiasm as he came through the front door. The response was disappointing. Jamie and Tammy were too focused on Grandma Pat and Grandpa Harry to even notice his arrival. He got a hello from the grandparents, but they were enjoying the kids' attention too much to say much more.

"Hi, honey," Carol said without even looking up from her reading.

Ray was eager to find out where they were going for their surprise funday. "So where are we headed this time?" he asked.

Carol said, "Pack your swimming suit; it will be warm." Since June in New Jersey can be quite warm, this was no hint. "We leave at five."

Early the following morning, Ray and Carol stood at the airline ticket counter. Being seasoned travelers, neither of them would check any luggage. They had enough clothes for five days in a warm climate.

"This is a surprise trip for my husband," Carol said to the woman at the ticket counter. "Can we keep the final destination a secret from him?"

The woman nodded and smiled at Ray. "Just let me see your ID, sir. You can have a seat over there." She pointed to a chair well out of earshot.

As they boarded the jet, Ray knew the first stop would be Florida, but he didn't know if that would be the final destination or just the point of changing planes. When the jet reached cruising altitude, Ray adjusted his seat into the reclining position.

"I have to hand it to you, Carol. I have no idea where we're going."

"So how did you do yesterday reviewing our dream list?" she asked. "And did you have any thoughts on what it cost?"

Ray smiled as he remembered opening Carol's sealed note on the train. "That was an enlightening assignment. I was amazed. Things that seemed impossible a year ago are realities for us now. Getting everything done daily, accomplishing more, reducing stress, experiencing more meaning and happiness—we're living our dream list. We even have some things that are not on the list, like overcoming interruptions and balancing our business and personal lives. And it cost me nothing but a willingness to change and give myself the three focus periods."

"What's incredible to me," said Carol, "is we've gone beyond our ideal professional and personal dream list on several levels."

Ray was intrigued by Carol's comment and turned in his seat so he could see her full face. "How so?" he asked.

"Remember when Mike Hall shared with us how he used to come home so tired and stressed out that sometimes he yelled at the people he loved? His problem was he could not see how his moment-to-moment actions were taking him to what he *really* wanted. When he used the Aligned Thinking tools to change that, he came home with more energy and was much more satisfied. I feel it is happening to us. What do you think?"

"You're right," said Ray.

"Plus," Carol continued, "there's our relationship. In the past, it seemed like the stress of our business lives and the lack of family and personal time were driving us apart. Now that we have a weekly family day and the quarterly funday for purpose, it's brought us all closer together."

"I agree," said Ray. For a moment they sat in silence. Then Ray added, "Another very satisfying aspect is how we have been able to help others to use the Aligned Thinking tools. At work, you helped your salespeople. I've shared the tools with many, including Ted Roland and his new hires. Our friends have appreciated our sharing. And our kids!"

They both laughed. Carol added, "After the kids used the tools to shape us up, I believe they started using the tools in their schoolwork."

Ray nodded. "I remember Coach saying that there's little in life more fulfilling than sharing our best with those we care about. He was right.

"I see what you mean about this going beyond our dream list." The silence intensified Ray's feelings of appreciation as he gazed out the airplane window. A layer of clouds hovered over the earth like a white blanket shining in the sun. He felt that their lives shared that shine.

The flight was a pleasant one. As the plane began its slow

descent, Carol looked up from her reading and said, "Ray, it just occurred to me that one of the most exciting values from Aligned Thinking, one I'd never even dreamed of—"

The pilot over the PA system interrupted her. "Good afternoon, ladies and gentlemen. We'll be landing in Miami in approximately seven minutes. Please turn off all electrical devices and return your seats to their upright positions."

"Perfect timing," Carol said with a smile. "You'll appreciate what I was going to say more after we catch our connecting flight."

"You're teasing me," Ray said.

"I know. Don't you love it?" Carol's eyes sparkled with mischief. Ray admitted to himself that this trip was shaping up to be even better than his ski trip to Vermont, though he was far from admitting it to Carol.

"Barbados!" Ray could hardly believe their destination as he boarded the connecting flight in Miami. "This is too much."

"Remember the last time we were in Barbados?" asked Carol.

"How could I forget? It was our honeymoon." The memories flooded back to Ray. Sadly, not all of them were blissful. "We were both too preoccupied with work."

Carol agreed. "To be honest, I think we had a pretty miserable time, focusing on everything but each other and our honeymoon. Remember how you told Woody that you wished you could do it all over again? Well, now you can."

Ray took Carol's hand and said, "Starting this moment, we can celebrate life all weekend long and do it together." The joy in her eyes soothed his guilt for letting so many romantic moments slide by without focusing on her.

The engines roared, preparing for take-off.

"You were about to share how Aligned Thinking has taken us to another level that you never dreamed of. What was it?" asked Ray.

"You just said it," Carol said tenderly. "Starting this moment, we can celebrate life all weekend long and beyond and do it *together!*"

Ray was thrilled to find out that Carol had arranged for them to stay in the same cottage they'd stayed in on their honeymoon. It was situated at the edge of the resort with a mile of white sand beach stretching beyond that point. When they arrived, not another person was in sight.

Exhausted after eleven hours and nearly two thousand miles of traveling, they lay down for a romantic nap together. As she had done so many times before, Carol slept on Ray's left shoulder. He looked affectionately at his wife, thinking of the many times in the past when his mind had not been in the right place—when she should have been his MIN and was not.

I feel so lucky I get this chance to do it over, he thought.

Carol and Ray napped for an hour. When they awoke, the sun still had more than an hour's warmth in it.

"Let's go sit on the beach and watch the sunset," said Carol as she headed for the cottage door.

Ray said, "Sure. Be there in a minute." He quickly wrote a note and put it in his pocket, then jogged to catch up with Carol.

Carol spread a towel on the white sand along the crescent beach. They settled down, taking in the beauty before them.

She turned to Ray and asked, "What did you write?"

Ray pulled the paper from his pocket and said, "With this second chance you've given me, I want to get it right this time."

Ray gave the note to Carol. It read:

My MIN is to enjoy the warm sun, cool breeze, and beautiful blue of the water and sky. But most of all, my MIN is my wonderful life partner, who creates unbelievably romantic surprises. She makes the future brilliant as we celebrate life this moment together.

CHAPTER TWENTY-TWO

A Life Better Than a Dream Come True

THE GLOW of their second honeymoon was still shining in Ray and Carol's eyes three weeks later as they sat around Coach Eric's large oak table. On the table was a very smartly wrapped package—possibly a present.

Ray and Carol had planned this meeting down to the last detail, rehearsing their script. They wanted to say thanks to Coach Eric in the most memorable, meaningful way.

As they had designed the tribute, Ray began, "Coach, a little more than a year ago, we came to you in desperation. We absolutely did not believe that we could align every action with what we really want, let alone have every action take us back to what we really want. In fact, at that time we only had a vague idea of what we really wanted. To live as Aligned Thinkers was way beyond what we thought possible."

"That's the truth," Carol affirmed.

"You asked us to write what we wanted our dream life to be," Ray continued. "You told us we could live our ideal professional and personal lives by becoming Aligned Thinkers.

The day you told us that at this table, it seemed so hard to believe.

"Using the Aligned Thinking tools, especially the MIN Secret, it has been much easier than we thought. With your help and the MIN Secret, we are not only enjoying living our ideal professional and personal lives, we have met or exceeded our ideals or dream life in at least four areas. We're forever grateful to you."

"Four levels beyond?" Coach repeated. "Tell me the four."

Carol spoke up, following their script. "Level 1: by aligning our actions to what we really want, we have more energy at the end of the day.

"Level 2: we no longer let the stress of business life detract from our personal life. By setting personal priorities regularly we now enjoy family time—especially the funday for purpose. We have a professional-personal balance.

"Level 3: we have shared these tools with fellow employees, friends, and our kids, the latter giving us more support than we expected."

Coach led the laughter as they all recalled how Tammy and Jamie helped Ray and Carol shape up in ways they had not anticipated.

Ray added, "Seriously, Coach, you said one of the most satisfying things we can do is help others. We believe we have helped people make significant life changes."

Coach affirmed proudly, "I think you're right."

"The final level," Carol continued, "is our ability to celebrate our life and our freedom in a very meaningful way. Ray and I both feel that when we are totally involved in our MIN with complete focus, there is no better way to celebrate life."

As planned, Ray added the final line. "What helps make this better than a dream come true is Carol and I can now celebrate life in this way together."

Ray gave Carol a very meaningful hug. Then it was Carol's turn. "We thank you for the gift of Aligned Thinking, especially for its *simple elegance*." She handed Coach the present.

Swallowing a lump in his throat, Coach Eric unwrapped the gift—a beautiful copper plaque.

**The Simple Elegance
of Aligned Thinking**

What's my
MIN,
related to what
I *really* want?

**MIN Secret
"Most Important Now" Secret**

Coach Eric lovingly studied the copper plaque. With a little crack in his voice, he said softly, "You two make me feel so proud."

"We have a plaque for everyone who helped," said Ray. "It's going to be fun delivering them."

Coach opened his mouth to speak, but just then his telephone began to ring. "Excuse me," he said, "do you mind if I get that?"

Ray and Carol assured him it was fine. "Hello? Oh, hi, Art. Um-hm." A concerned look came over Coach's face. "No, that's not good. Um-hm . . . yes . . . I understand. Yes, I'm sure I can help you with that. Listen, I have company right now. Can I call you back? All right. Talk to you soon."

Coach hung up the phone and turned to Ray and Carol. "Sorry. Thanks for your patience."

"No big deal," said Ray.

"Is everything okay?" asked Carol. "It sounded like the caller had a serious problem."

Coach chuckled. "You're right, Carol. He did. That was a new acquaintance of mine, Art. He and his wife, Flo, are very frustrated. He says they have too much to do. They don't seem to be able to get enough accomplished. They have too many interruptions. Not enough time with their family. Art said he was feeling like he had very little control over his life, and the whole thing doesn't seem to have much meaning anymore."

By now all three of them were grinning. Coach continued, "Do you guys know anyone who might be able to help them?"

Ray's smile was as wide as his heart was full. "Tell them to come over and see us. We will be so honored to help."

THE END

Although this is the end of this part of Ray and Carol's journey, it's only the beginning of Ray and Carol's pilgrimage as Aligned Thinkers to a life better than their dream come true:

A journey on which they will be able to make every moment count, celebrate life each moment together, and receive the rich reward of sharing their life with others.

A journey to a life as successful people on their way to getting what they really want from life and work.

MY MENTOR, Ken Blanchard, shared with me how to get more from a book or seminar: during or immediately after reading the book or attending the seminar, write down a couple of key ideas that you want to remember. I suggest you do this now.

Idea 1, page _____ topic _____

_____

_____

Idea 2, page _____ topic _____

_____

_____

Idea 3, page _____ topic _____

_____

_____

Who are the key people in your life you would like to share the benefits of Aligned Thinking with?

Staff _____	Spouse _____
Direct Reports _____	Son(s) _____
Boss _____	Daughter(s) _____
Coworkers _____	Mother _____
Peers _____	Father _____
Clients _____	Relatives _____
Others _____	Friends _____

ACKNOWLEDGMENTS

IT IS difficult to adequately acknowledge the huge influence Ken Blanchard is in my life. When I had difficulty with my doctorate, he came to help. After twenty years of my trying to write this book alone, it was his guidance, coaching, and encouragement that got the job done. When the manuscript needed help, he discovered miracle worker and editor par excellence Martha Lawrence, who worked her magic. I salute his entire staff, especially Dotti Hamilt and Richard Andrews.

I am deeply grateful to my parents, Ray and Eleanor Steffen, my father- and mother-in-law, Harry and Pat Karp, and my many relatives, especially Father Valerian Schott, OFM, and Father Julius Schott, OFM, for the great environment they provided for these ideas to grow.

Then I must thank my wife, Carol, who not only read, corrected, and reread the manuscript many times, but also gave her insight and patience in helping to make multiple decisions about every part of the book. Without her, writing this book would have been a totally different experience.

I acknowledge my children, Ray, Eric, Alanna, Jamie, and Tammy, for their positive encouragement and understanding when the book took me away from supporting them.

I want to acknowledge Woody Bliss's contribution to the Aligned Thinking process. He helped me appreciate the universality of Aligned Thinking when he used it with his international senior IBM salespeople; with his wife, Prue, and high

school daughters, Suzie and Barbara; and now as first select-
man of Weston, Connecticut.

I owe Gary Polakoff, a twenty-two-year alumnus of the
Aligned Thinking process, an ongoing debt of gratitude. For
years he has daily encouraged me as he helps me be what I
wish I were and fear I am not.

I want to recognize Emilio DeLia's superb coaching,
which helped me clarify the Aligned Thinking process as my
passion.

I wish to acknowledge the following clients, who have be-
come my friends and supporters in this effort: Peter Donovan,
Rick Chase, Roger Henson, Dennis Lauterbach, Jake
Monaghan, and Dan Wiersma.

Right from the very beginning of Aligned Thinking,
many colleagues have helped develop the process, taught
the process, and been a source of never-ending encouragement. These are Erika and Sheldon Hearst, Jon Barb,
Duncan Rowles, Jim White, Dave Gilman, Bob Arnold,
Sue Towsley, and Tad Muszynski.

I am grateful to Paul Mitchell and Dom Esolda. In the
first of eight drafts this time around, they insisted that this
book deserved to be published.

I must recognize publisher Steve Piersanti for helping the
insights in this book take a huge step to achieving the elegant simplicity that it has. I also want to acknowledge Jeevan
Sivasubramaniam, Kristen Frantz, Michael Crowley, and
their team at Berrett-Koehler for what they have done and
are doing to help this book achieve its full potential.

Most importantly, I must thank my Higher Spirit. As the
preface states, for twenty years and fifteen drafts this book
went nowhere. My Higher Spirit seemed to say, "Give me
the book. You're responsible for listening and following

guidance. I'll be responsible for results." Frequently, when my editor and I got stuck, we went to him. To date, the results of his generosity have exceeded my expectations. I'm deeply grateful. I'm excited about what the future holds with his being responsible for the future results.

DR. STEFFEN is available for keynote presentations. Several of his more requested presentations are

- The Simple Elegance of Aligned Thinking
- I Never Get Everything Done: Five Simple Steps to Change This Forever
- How to Take Your Culture and Profitability Up a Level or Two

For a complete list, see "Presentations" on the Web site given below.

He has delivered Aligned Thinking™ and Successful Partnering™ seminars and webinars to 140 Fortune 500 companies. (The list is on the Web site.) For those who would like the guidance of Coach Eric immediately in their lives but cannot travel, Dr. Steffen offers a weekly course delivered conveniently to your computer, entitled, "Five Simple Coaching Sessions to Implement Aligned Thinking."

He is also available for coaching individuals and groups. SSA International offers a certification program to teachers and coaches who want to offer Aligned Thinking and Successful Partnering to their own clients or company.

203-740-8400
www.SSAinternational.com

AUTHOR'S GIFT TO YOU FOR
READING *ALIGNED THINKING*

Even though Aligned Thinking is elegantly simple, it is challenging to create new habits so that you can enjoy a *quantum leap* in your motivation, accomplishment, and satisfaction. To make it as easy, simple, and quick as possible for you to implement these new habits, I have created the following gift for you:

A personal analysis of how you can align
every action to what you *really* want.

This personal analysis will show you both your strengths and growth opportunities.
   This gift also includes

- Three months' virtual personal coaching to implement Aligned Thinking

- Ten monthly sessions of the Professional/ Personal Growth Kit

TO RECEIVE THIS FREE GIFT IMMEDIATELY, GO TO
www.SSAinternational.com/personalanalysis
Use personal analysis free access code 8151225.

TO RECEIVE AN INFORMATION KIT
OR TO CONTACT US
CALL: **203-740-8400**
E-MAIL: **rjsteffen@SSAinternational.com**

DR. R. JAMES (JIM) STEFFEN, president and founder of Steffen, Steffen & Associates, Inc. (SSA International), is an internationally known author, speaker, consultant, and trainer. He is recognized as an expert in Aligned Thinking and Time Mastery, leadership, productivity, and Successful Partnering, which focuses on creating very satisfied, loyal customers and employees. Because of his record of accomplishment, he has had opportunities to work with more than 140 Fortune 500 companies. (The list is available at www.SSAinternational.com.)

Dr. Steffen has four degrees: one undergraduate degree in philosophy from Quincy University and one in theology from St. Joseph Seminary, a master's degree in math from the University of Notre Dame, and a doctorate in education from the University of Massachusetts, where he led the Leadership Lab.

He created the Aligned Thinking seminar and ten other seminars. They are built on a triple set of skills:

- *Research* to discover the root cause or growth opportunities
- *Creativity* to solve the problem or use the opportunity
- *Speaking and coaching* to teach or train others to teach and deliver the solutions and to create measurable, repeatable results

People love stories. Jim is a storyteller from beginning to end. He has more than thirty years of success stories to share and is an award-winning presenter.

ABOUT BERRETT-KOEHLER PUBLISHERS

BERRETT-KOEHLER is an independent publisher dedicated to an ambitious mission: Creating a World That Works for All.

We believe that to truly create a better world, action is needed at all levels—individual, organizational, and societal. At the individual level, our publications help people align their lives and work with their deepest values. At the organizational level, our publications promote progressive leadership and management practices, socially responsible approaches to business, and humane and effective organizations. At the societal level, our publications advance social and economic justice, shared prosperity, sustainable development, and new solutions to national and global issues.

We publish groundbreaking books focused on each of these levels. To further advance our commitment to positive change at the societal level, we have recently expanded our line of books in this area and are calling this expanded line "BK Currents."

A major theme of our publications is "Opening Up New Space." They challenge conventional thinking, introduce new points of view, and offer new alternatives for change. Their common quest is changing the underlying beliefs, mindsets, institutions, and structures that keep generating the same cycles of problems, no matter who our leaders are or what improvement programs we adopt.

We strive to practice what we preach—to operate our publishing company in line with the ideas in our books. At the core of our approach is stewardship, which we define as a deep sense of responsibility to administer the company for the benefit of all of our "stakeholder" groups: authors, customers, employees, investors, service providers, and the communities and environment around us. We seek to establish a partnering relationship with each stakeholder that is open, equitable, and collaborative.

We are gratified that thousands of readers, authors, and other friends of the company consider themselves to be part of the "BK Community." We hope that you, too, will join our community and connect with us through the ways described on our website at www.bkconnection.com.

BE CONNECTED

Visit Our Website

Go to www.bkconnection.com to read exclusive previews and excerpts of new books, find detailed information on all Berrett-Koehler titles and authors, browse subject-area libraries of books, and get special discounts.

Subscribe to Our Free E-Newsletter

Be the first to hear about new publications, special discount offers, exclusive articles, news about bestsellers, and more! Get on the list for our free e-newsletter by going to www.bkconnection.com.

Participate in the Discussion

To see what others are saying about our books and post your own thoughts, check out our blogs at www.bkblogs.com.

Get Quantity Discounts

Berrett-Koehler books are available at quantity discounts for orders of ten or more copies. Please call us toll-free at (800) 929-2929 or email us at bkp.orders@aidcvt.com.

Host a Reading Group

For tips on how to form and carry on a book reading group in your workplace or community, see our website at www.bkconnection.com.

Join the BK Community

Thousands of readers of our books have become part of the "BK Community" by participating in events featuring our authors, reviewing draft manuscripts of forthcoming books, spreading the word about their favorite books, and supporting our publishing program in other ways. If you would like to join the BK Community, please contact us at bkcommunity@bkpub.com.